The author was born a son of the manse and as a medical student, became president of the Student Christian Movement at Liverpool University.

As a junior doctor, he was awarded the Royal Humane Society medal for bravery. He progressed to a career in orthopaedic surgery with qualifications, FRCS (Ed.), FRCS (Eng.) and MChOrth. He has a record of academic achievement having been Associate Professor at the Albert Einstein College of Medicine, New York and appointed Hunterian Professor at the Royal College of Surgeons, England for original research on adolescent hip disease. He was co-author of papers that established the Charnley hip replacement as the gold standard for several decades. He has been awarded an OBE for services to medicine.

It was only after his retirement as Consultant Orthopaedic Surgeon that he had the opportunity to reflect more deeply on his beliefs, particularly in the light of work by many eminent academics in recent decades.

Dedication

With love to Elizabeth without whose support this book would not have materialised.

Maldwyn Griffith

THE HISTORICAL JESUS

The Origins of Christian Belief

AUSTIN MACAULEY PUBLISHERS™

LONDON • CAMBRIDGE • NEW YORK • SHARJAH

A CIP catalogue record for this title is available from the British Library.

ISBN 9781787106925 (Paperback)
ISBN 9781787106932 (E-Book)

www.austinmacauley.com

First Published (2018)
Austin Macauley Publishers Ltd.
25 Canada Square
Canary Wharf
London
E14 5LQ

I know that most men – not only those considered clever, but even those who are very clever, and capable of understanding most difficult scientific, mathematical, or philosophic, problems – can seldom discern even the simplest and most obvious truth if it be such as obliges them to admit the falsity of conclusions they have formed, perhaps with much difficulty – conclusions of which they are proud, which they have taught to others, and on which they have built their lives.

(Tolstoy, *What is Art?,* p.154)

Contents

Introduction   13
I   19

  History of the Jews   19

II   42

  Religious Practice in Palestine at the time of Jesus   42

III   61

  Introduction to The New Testament   61

IV   70

  The Birth of Jesus   70

V   80

  John the Baptist and Jesus   80

VI   86

  Jesus the Charismatic Exorcist and Healer   86

VII   104

  The Teaching of Jesus   104

VIII   121

  Jesus' Last Week in Jerusalem   121

IX   143

  The Resurrection of Jesus   143

X   155

  The Disciples' Response to their Experience of the Resurrection   155

XI   160

  Paul's Influence on the Early Church   160

XII   185

  The Concept of God Incarnate   185

XIII   201
  Reflections on the Nicene Creed   201
Conclusion   211
Works Cited   217
Further Reading   219

Palestine in the time of Jesus

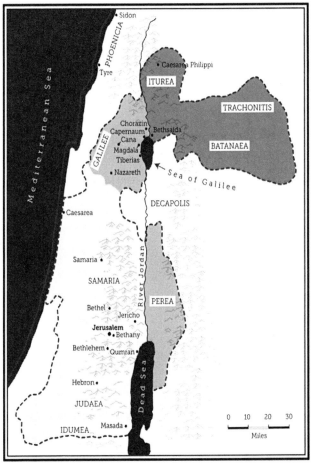

To Archelaus

To Herod Antipas

To Phillip

- - - - Border of Herod's realm

Introduction

I was born a son of the Manse and have maintained a connection with the Presbyterian Church all my life, albeit with some doubts. The abiding influence of one's upbringing was brought home to me recently after a conducted tour of Martin Luther's home in Wittenberg. He was, of course, a seminal figure in the Protestant Reformation and in 1517 nailed his *Ninety-Five Theses* to the door of All Saints' Church. In particular he objected to the sale of indulgences by the Roman Catholic Church that could absolve men of their sins and buy salvation. Afterwards, over a coffee, a group of us were discussing our visit when a Roman Catholic lady said, 'I wish I had been born a Lutheran'. The ties to her upbringing remained a dominant factor in her life. Early influences are a fact of life, and I was similarly affected by my Presbyterian roots.

As a young man I was also influenced by Dietrich Bonhoeffer and his posthumously published *Letters and Papers from Prison*. Bonhoeffer was born in Poland in 1906, to a large and distinguished family. His father was a professor of neurology and psychiatry and later moved to Berlin. Bonhoeffer studied theology at the University of Tubingen in Germany. He was a brilliant student, and by the age of twenty-two he was awarded the degree of Doctor of Theology from Berlin University. In 1930, he accepted a postgraduate teaching fellowship at the Union Theological Seminary in New York. Whilst there, he taught at a Baptist Church Sunday school in Harlem. With his privileged background and time spent in the ivory towers of academic theology, this exposure to the harsh realities facing an oppressed people was to influence the rest of his life.

On returning to Berlin, Bonhoeffer was ordained at the Old Prussian Union Evangelical Church. On 30 January 1933, the Nazi party gained power and Hitler was appointed Fuhrer two days later. A radio broadcast by Bonhoeffer warning the nation of the potential threat posed by Hitler was cut off the air in mid-sentence. In April 1933, Bonhoeffer was the first to resist Hitler's persecution of the Jews, maintaining that the church must not simply bandage the victims crushed under the wheel of state machinery, but jam the spoke in the wheel itself. In July 1933, Hitler imposed new church elections for officials of the Protestant-established churches, ensuring, through a process of rigging, that the majority were Nazi supporters.

In September 1933, non-Aryans were prohibited from taking parish posts. When Bonhoeffer was offered a parish post in eastern Berlin, he refused on principle. Later, Bonhoeffer was to become a leading member of an underground Christian opposition to Hitler known as the Confessing Church. He spent two years in London as pastor to two German-speaking Protestant churches. It was his hope that the worldwide ecumenical movement would support the Confessing Church. Soon after his return to Germany, the Gestapo closed one of Bonhoeffer's seminaries and arrested twenty-seven pastors and former students. In 1939, at the invitation of the Union Theological Seminary, he returned to America. There he could have lived a comfortable life advancing his understanding of theology and ethics. However, he could not desert his fellow Germans who opposed Hitler. He returned to Germany on 20 June 1939.

Bonhoeffer's brother-in-law, Hans von Dohnányi, was a Supreme Court Advisor. He helped Bonhoeffer to join the *Abwehr*, a German military intelligence organisation staffed largely by civilians. It was thought that through his international contacts he could potentially provide useful information. However, Bonhoeffer and other members of his family were part of a covert group of conspirators planning the overthrow of Hitler. He lived a life of camouflage and deceit. His visits to Norway, Sweden and Switzerland were disguised as legitimate intelligence activities for the *Abwehr*. On 5 April 1943, he and

Dohnányi were arrested, not on account of their conspiratorial activities, but owing to the efforts of the Gestapo headquarters to prove that certain rules and agreements between them and *Abwehr* had been broken. Their intention was to gain control of the *Abwehr*. He was held at Tegel military prison.

On 20 July 1944, a plot to kill Hitler failed and in September, secret *Abwehr* documents linking Bonhoeffer to the conspiracy were discovered. He was transferred to the Gestapo's high-security prison. In February 1945 he was secretly transferred to Buchenwald concentration camp and finally to Flossenburg concentration camp. On 4 April 1945, the diaries of Admiral Wilhelm Canaris, head of the *Abwehr*, were discovered, revealing the extent of the conspiracy. Bonhoeffer and six other conspirators, including Canaris, were executed by hanging on 9 April 1945, just two weeks before the Americans liberated the camp. Bonhoeffer's brother and two brothers-in-law were also executed.

Bonhoeffer was a great intellectual, a man of immense courage and deep spirituality. He struggled with what it meant to be a Christian in Nazi Germany. He maintained that Christians should not retreat from the world but act in it. Man had "come of age" and we should no longer use God as a stopgap for the incompleteness of our knowledge. He inspired Martin Luther King Jr., and had a great influence on American civil rights and the anti-Apartheid movement in South Africa. He is commemorated in the gallery of twentieth century martyrs at Westminster Abbey and on a German postage stamp issued in 1995.

My personal admiration of Bonhoeffer was enhanced when, as President of the Student Christian movement at Liverpool University, I had the privilege of meeting Pastor Eberhard Bethge, to whom Bonhoeffer had written the *Letters and Papers from Prison*. It enhanced my father's principle beliefs in morality, compassion and a positive attitude to life and the world. One of Bonhoeffer's poems, *Christians and Unbelievers* has remained with me.

Men go to God when they are sore bestead,

Pray to him for succour, for his peace, for bread,
For mercy for them sick, sinning or dead;
All men do so, Christian and unbelieving.

Men go to God when he is sore bestead,
Find him poor and scorned, without shelter or bread,
Whelmed under the weight of the wicked, the weak, the dead;
Christians stand by God in his hour of grieving (Bonhoeffer, 1953, p. 174).

This poem was written to reflect his understanding of the meaning of Jesus' crucifixion and was not a simply humanist approach to life.

The influence of my father and Bonhoeffer gave me a moral compass which has influenced my decisions and actions throughout my life, albeit without any absolute certainty. When I retired from my life as an orthopaedic surgeon I began to think more deeply as to what I really believed. I could have cherry-picked parts of the Bible that best fitted my preconceptions, but this would have been a subjective exercise and of no real value to anyone except myself. Christians frequently disagree over the interpretation or relative relevance of individual verses in the Bible. Too often one or two verses have been taken out of context to justify individual prejudices in the name of religious dogma and divine authority. We have witnessed discrimination against race, colour, gender, class, religion or sexual orientation based on Biblical authority. This is not another attempt to interpret the Bible as relevant to the twenty-first century, important a task as that may be.

Advances in human knowledge and understanding are often dependent on challenges to traditional beliefs. In what follows, my approach has been to attempt to turn the clock back about two thousand years in order to understand the motivation and rationale of the original authors of the New Testament. To do this one has to place their writing in the context of the religious, cultural and historical influences prevailing at that time. Christian belief is based on the historical figure of Jesus.

However, the New Testament contains differing accounts of his life that reflect evolving thoughts on his significance. To take one example, according to Matthew, after the birth of Jesus in Bethlehem, his parents fled to Egypt to avoid the wrath of Herod. On the other hand, according to Luke, they went to the Temple in Jerusalem to give thanks to the Lord. How credible is John's account of the crucifixion of Jesus on Thursday afternoon before the Passover meal? I believe that we can gain an understanding of these contradictory accounts by examining the authors' own underlying preconceptions.

In order to facilitate a deeper understanding of the New Testament, the first two chapters are devoted to the history of the Jews and their religious practice at the time of Jesus. The historical and cultural factors that could have had an influence on the authors of the New Testament are largely but not exclusively taken from two of Flavius Josephus' books, *Bellum Judaicum* or *Books of History of the Jewish War Against the Romans*, c. 75 AD, and *Antiquitates Judaicae* loosely translated as *Antiquities of the Jews* (c. 94 AD). Josephus was born in 37 AD to a priestly family and after formal training became a Pharisee. After some time in Rome he returned to Palestine in 66 AD. He tried to persuade the Jews of the futility of war against the Romans but to no avail. With the inevitability of war, Josephus was appointed commander of Jewish forces in Galilee. He was taken prisoner by the Romans but managed to ingratiate himself with the emperor Vespasian and spent the rest of his life in Rome. He was given a pension and a house. Here he composed his work towards the end of the first century AD. We know more about Palestine in the first century AD than we do about any other part of the Roman Empire during that period. His history is presented predominantly from the Jewish point of view.

Biblical quotations are taken from the Revised Standard Version with a few from the Jerusalem Bible credited with the initials JB. The land of the Jews comprised various provinces and for reasons of simplicity I have on occasions used Palestine as a generic term to cover Jewish territory. In today's terminology it comprises both Israel and Palestine. The northern province of Israel was conquered by the Assyrians in 734 BC and its people scattered. The name Israel was reintroduced in 1947 with the proposal to create a Jewish territory within Palestine.

All researchers are dependent on those who have gone before. During the last fifty years, academics on both sides of the Atlantic have made significant contributions to a re-appraisal of the New Testament. This book would not have been possible without their scholarly work which I acknowledge in my bibliography. The opinions, omissions and errors, however, are my responsibility.

I

History of the Jews

Early Accounts

Two thousand years ago the Jews would have been familiar with their history through the regular readings in the synagogues from their Hebrew Scriptures, represented as the Old Testament in the Christian Bible. The Hebrew Scriptures gives the story of the Jewish nation not as history per se, but as an account of how they believed God had intervened in their history. It involved deliverance and redemption but also suffering and exile. Also, it addresses some of the profound questions about human experience through stories or myths that would have been comprehensible at the time. Even today, the collective consciousness of individual nations includes their own myths. All that is necessary at this stage is to draw a broad-brush picture of Jewish history as revealed in the Hebrew Scriptures, supplemented by other contemporary texts.

The Bible begins with God's creation of the physical universe, then of mankind through Adam and Eve. They contravene God's command and eat of the tree of knowledge of good and evil (Genesis 3.1–7). They are banished from the idyllic Garden of Eden to live a life of toil and painful childbearing. Cain, their eldest son, murders his brother, Abel, in rage. Some generations later, 'The Lord saw that the wickedness of man was great on the earth,' and decided that he would:

blot out man whom I have created from the face of the ground, man and beast and creeping things and birds of the air, for I am sorry that I have made them (Genesis 6.5–7).

The world was flooded and all perished except for one favoured family, that of Noah who had built an ark. After the flood, God vows never to destroy the earth again and creates a rainbow as a symbol and a reminder to both himself and mankind of the promise (Genesis 9.8–17). In spite of this, neither Noah nor his successors amend their ways. The story of the Tower of Babel is an explanation for the diversity of language and the final disintegration of order and unity described in the primal act of creation. Similar accounts occur in Babylonian literature and the Tower of Babel has similarities to the ziggurats in the Tigris-Euphrates valley.

God again attempts to create a moral society, initially through the family of one man called Abraham. He was born and brought up in Ur of the Chaldaeans in the south-east of Mesopotamia. His father Terah decided to leave Ur to go to Canaan (the region between the river Jordan and the Mediterranean corresponding roughly to the modern states of Lebanon, Israel and the Palestinian territories). He was accompanied by Abraham, Abraham's wife Sarah and Abraham's nephew, Lot. They travelled through Mesopotamia to Haran in the north-west of the country, now south-east Turkey, where they settled and prospered. Terah died in Haran.

Now, the Lord said to Abraham, 'Go from your country and your kindred and your father's house to the land that I will show you. And I will make of you a great nation, and I will bless you, and make your name great, so that you will be a blessing. I will bless those who bless you, and him who curses you I will curse; and through you all the families of the earth will be blessed' (Genesis 12.1–3).

The converse of the agreement or covenant was that they must walk before God and be blameless (Genesis 17.1), that as a sign of the covenant all males will be circumcised (Genesis

17.11) and that they should 'keep the way of the Lord by doing righteousness and justice' (Genesis 18.19).

Abraham settled in Canaan but famine persuaded him to go to Egypt. There, Sarah was seduced by Pharaoh and God inflicted severe plagues on Pharaoh's household. Abraham returned to Canaan with significant possessions. He and Lot, his nephew, had large herds and decided to separate. Lot choose the fertile Jordan plain and settled in Sodom. Abraham moved to Hebron.

Abraham had no heir so Sarah suggested he should have a child with Hagar, their Egyptian slave-girl. Hagar bore him a son that they named Ishmael. Later Sarah, although past her menopause, gave birth to Isaac. Hagar and Ishmael were dismissed from the household and lived in the wilderness until Hagar found an Egyptian wife for Ishmael.

One night, Lot entertained two strangers, who were angels in disguise. They were disturbed by the men of Sodom asking that the strangers be sent out so that they could sexually abuse them. Lot refused but offered to send out his two virgin daughters. They were not interested in his daughters, a fight broke out but the door was eventually locked. The men of Sodom were struck with blindness. In the morning, the strangers persuaded Lot and his family to leave Sodom. They fled to Zoar, but in the process the wife of Lot contravened instructions from the strangers not to look back and turned into a pillar of salt. Brimstone and fire rained on Sodom and Gomorrah, devastating the whole area. Lot, fearful of the reaction of the people of Zoar, went to live in a cave. Both daughters became pregnant by their father. The eldest named her son Moab and became the ancestor of the Moabites. The younger named her son Ben-Ammi, forerunner of the Ammonites.

Abraham is held as the founding father of the Jewish, Christian and Islamic religions. He is portrayed as a righteous man who enjoyed close and constant communion with God. He is regarded as the first Hebrew and father of the Jewish people. God promises him that Isaac, his second, son would inherit the land of Canaan. The traditional Christian view is that God's promise to Abraham meant that through his seed all people of the earth would be blessed, hence the New Testament's genealogy of Jesus is traced back to Abraham. Moslems believe that Muhammad is his direct descendent through his first son, Ishmael. The traditional Moslem view is that Hagar and Ishmael went to live in the Mecca valley where God had taken care of them, revealing the sacred spring of Zamzam when they were dying of thirst. Abraham later visited them and with the help of Ishmael built the Ka'aba, the first temple of the one God. Today, the Ka'aba (translated as "The Cube") is a large masonry structure covered with black silk trimmed with gold at the centre of the Great Mosque in Mecca, Al-Masjid al-Haram. To Moslems it is the most sacred place on earth and they all face it during prayer. During the Hajj pilgrimage they walk seven times around the Ka'aba in an anti-clockwise direction.

Abraham probably lived sometime between the twentieth and nineteenth century BC. The account has no reference to any historical events that can be verified. It is the account of one family's devotion to one God. Maybe this is an approximate portrayal of his life. What is important is that two thousand years ago he was revered by the Jews as their founding father.

The narrative continues with accounts of the patriarchs, Isaac, Jacob and Joseph leading a nomadic life until they settle in Egypt. Eventually, under a new Pharaoh, probably Merneptah (c. 1236–1223 BC), the Egyptians 'made the people of Israel serve with rigor, and made their lives bitter with hard service, in mortar and brick, and in all kind of work in the field' (Exodus 1.13–14). God "remembers" his covenant and calls Moses to lead his people from slavery. Their escape from Egypt and their subsequent time as refugees in the Sinai desert left indelible images on their consciousness. God reveals his will to Israel by renewing his covenant (Exodus 34.10–37) and the Ten Commandments (Exodus 20.1–17). These were expounded in detailed instruction covering all aspects of social and moral behaviour in the second half of Exodus through Leviticus, Numbers and Deuteronomy. This was the Torah or "teaching". Although ascribed to Moses, much of the instruction was compiled much later.

Under the leadership of Joshua the Jews eventually settled in Canaan. The book of Joshua gives accounts of the river Jordan drying up to allow them to cross, and the walls of Jericho falling without a blow being struck and all Canaanites being killed. Other biblical accounts, however, suggest that there was probably no epic battle, rather a gradual assimilation over several generations as the nomadic Israelites became settled agriculturists. This was a loose amalgamation of twelve tribes, each descended from one of Jacob's sons. There was no capital, no high priest and no central shrine. 'In those days there was no king in Israel; every man did what was right in his own eyes' (Judg. 17.6). Their experiences in the desert and the teachings of Moses had become their conscience. They only had one ruler and that was God. This was the idealistic image portrayed.

The Jews were unhappy with this state of affairs and wished to appoint a king. They consulted Samuel, a priest, who warned them of the dangers of a monarchy (1 Sam. 8.11–18). They responded, 'No! But we will have a king over us, that we also may be like all the nations, and that our king may govern us and go out before us and fight our battles' (1 Samuel 8.19–20). Samuel anoints Saul King of Israel although he regards their request as 'great wickedness' (1 Samuel 12.17). He reaffirms God's constancy in spite of the people's disobedience.

It was Saul's successor, David, whose reign (c. 1010–970 BC) was regarded by future generations as the golden age. David united the tribes under his leadership, defeated their enemies and made Jerusalem the centre of political power and national worship by placing the Ark of the Covenant there. This was a wooden chest covered with gold, containing two tablets of stone on which the Ten Commandments were written. His son Solomon built the house of the Lord, the Temple. David's success was considered the result of his love of and obedience to God. Thus began a Davidic Messianic hope:

When your days are fulfilled and you lie down with your fathers, I will raise up your son after you, who shall come forth from your body, and I shall establish his kingdom… I will be his father, and he shall be my son (2 Sam. 7.12–16).

At the time, the hope was that one day a Jewish monarch would rule over the nations and lead them to acknowledge and worship their God, creator of the universe.

Following the death of Solomon, the tribes of Israel broke into two groups, ten in the northern territory, known as Israel, and two in the south, known as Judah. Each group had its own king but a common religion. However some turned to the worship of Baal with consequent persecution and massacres. Over the next two hundred years there was almost constant fighting between the northern and southern groups: 'There was war between Rehoboam and Jeroboam continually' (1 Kings 14.30). The Assyrians invaded the northern territories in 734 BC and scattered the conquered people in order to reduce the chance of revolt. These became known as the lost tribes of Israel.

It was the prophets who interpreted the political events in a religious context. Israel's suffering had a redemptive meaning. Through chastisement, Israel will repent and act with justice and righteousness. Israel's faithfulness to the Torah will bring peace to the whole world:

> From out of Zion shall go forth the law [Torah] and the word of the Lord from Jerusalem... Nation shall not lift sword against nation, neither shall they learn war any more (Isaiah 2.3–4).

This was a message of hope and expectation but this was not to be.

In 586 BC, the Babylonians under Nebuchadnezzar II invaded Israel and destroyed the first Temple. They deported fifteen thousand of the principal Israelites to Babylon. Ezekiel, a priest who was exiled to Babylon wrote of God's impending intervention:

> Behold, I am against you, O Gog, chief prince of Meshech and Tubal... You shall fall on the mountains of Israel, you and all your hordes and the peoples that are with you; I will give you to the birds of prey of every sort and to the wild beasts to be devoured (Ezekiel 39.1–7).

Ezekiel expected that there would be a battle that would result in the establishment of a divine kingdom and Israel's supremacy.

In 538 BC the Babylonian empire fell to Cyrus II of Persia. Cyrus, being tolerant of other religions – he was a Zoroastrian – allowed a small group of Jews to return to Jerusalem. The Temple was rebuilt and dedicated in 516 BC. It was a symbol of historical continuity with the past. Temple sacrifices could again be offered. This formed the focal point for Jews scattered around the Eastern Mediterranean, helping to preserve their identity. However, there was one area of controversy. Those Jews who had remained in the province of Samaria had their own site of worship at Sechem, and later in the third century BC built a temple on Mount Gerazim that rivalled Jerusalem's. The rivalry continued to the time of Jesus. Samaritans refused to receive Jesus, 'because his face was set toward Jerusalem' (Luke 9.53, John 4.20). The Samaritans regarded the first five books of the Old Testament, the Pentateuch, as the only valid scripture. The Jews regarded the Samaritans as being of mixed blood.

Jerusalem was completely disorganised socially and religiously. It was not until the time of the prophets Nehemiah and Ezra (c. 446–430 BC) that stability and orthodox religious observance were restored. The Babylonian Jews gradually returned. They were relatively few in number and their territory was limited to within ten to fifteen miles of Jerusalem. As part of the Persian Empire, there followed a century of relative stability when they preserved their exclusiveness and maintained their traditions.

From Alexander the Great to 135 AD

The conquests of Alexander the Great between 334 and 323 BC ended the Persian Empire. His empire encompassed what we now call Turkey, Syria, Palestine, Jordan, Egypt, Iraq, Iran, Afghanistan, Pakistan and Kashmir. Jerusalem seems to have come peaceably into his possession. The Hellenistic world had been created, Greek language, literature and worship became widely known. Whilst Athens remained an important cultural centre, the newer cities of Antioch, Pergamum and above all Alexandria predominated. Alexandria became the international centre for learning and the arts. There was a large Jewish population in Alexandria. It was here in 270 BC that the Pentateuch, the first five books of the Old Testament, was first translated into Greek. Some Jews were influenced by the new civilisation. Greek thought no longer centred on the city and civic virtue, but looked inward on the individual and outward on the world. Stoics and Epicureans were agreed that there was a Law of Nature above the laws of nations and that duty is the same for all men. Pride in Greek blood gave way to pride in Greek civilisation.

After Alexander's death, a period of fierce fighting ensued amongst his generals for possession of his empire. Israel found itself a contested territory between two kingdoms, Syria to the north and Egypt to the south. In 301 BC, Egypt, under the command of Ptolemy I, secured Israel. At first the Jews were content and were able to continue their traditions. They prospered and many lived in Egypt.

The Syrians (or Seleucid empire) were not content and, though defeated in 217 BC, persisted and in 198 BC, gained a decisive victory over the Egyptians and took control of Israel. The Syrian capital, Antioch, was Hellenistic and its influence on the Jews created a powerful Greek thinking party in Jerusalem. They introduced a Greek institution, the gymnasium. Here boys and youths were educated. Part of the curriculum involved exercise in the nude. Jewish males had been circumcised but those brought up in Greek culture, believing in a sound mind in a sound body, regarded this as disgusting mutilation. Some Jews tried to disguise their circumcision thus denying their covenant with God (1 Macc. 1.14 JB).

Conflicts developed with those who cherished the old ideals and the righteousness of the Law. Orias, the high priest and leader of the orthodox party, drove the Hellenising adherents out of Jerusalem. Civil war broke out between the two factions. The king of Syria, Antiochus IV Epiphanes, intervened with merciless severity, not only to extinguish the revolt but also to try to prevent its recurrence. In 170 BC he removed the treasure and sacred vessels from the Temple, installed an image of the Greek god Zeus and recast the service according to Greek beliefs, including the sacrifice of pigs, an anathema to the Jews. Those who persisted in their Jewish practices and refused to sacrifice to Zeus were tortured or killed. Many of the old patriotic party, now called the Hasidim or righteous ones gave up their lives rather than betray their principles. Others escaped to more remote parts of the country. Jerusalem became a Greek city with a Syrian garrison.

The Hasmonean Dynasty (The Maccabees)

Mattathias, a member of the highly respected Hasmonean priestly family, led a revolt. Having refused to offer a heathen sacrifice he saw another Jew doing so at the behest of Apelles, a Syrian officer. He killed them both. Fleeing to the wilderness with his five sons, he gathered others around him. They were like-minded and observed the Law even to the point of refusing to defend themselves on the Sabbath lest they defile the holy day. Josephus recounts how the Syrians:

> ... fought against them on the Sabbath-day, and they burnt them as they were in the caves, without resistance, and without so much as [the Jews] stopping up the entrances of the caves... There were about a thousand, with their wives and children, who were smothered and died in these caves: but many of those that escaped joined themselves to Mattathias, and appointed him to be their ruler, who taught them to fight even on the Sabbath-day (Josephus, *Antiquities* 12:6.2).

Mattathias formed an army and won some skirmishes but he died in 166 BC. One of his five sons, Judas Maccabaeus, or the "hammer of the heathen", became commander and in less than two years, by a series of remarkable victories, almost cleared Judah of the Syrians. The Temple was rededicated on 25 December 165 BC and its worship restored. The event is commemorated to this day by the Feast of Dedication (John 10.22). Judas Maccabaeus died in battle. His two brothers,

27

Jonathan, and later, Simon continued the struggle. An independent Jewish state emerged in 140 BC and the first Jewish coins were struck in Simon's name.

The Hasmoneans (nicknamed the Maccabees) had established a new dynasty. They ruled as high priests and eventually took on the title king. Judah's narrow limits were extended to the north to encompass Samaria and Galilee and to the south Idumaea, biblical Edom. In Samaria they destroyed the temple on Mount Gerazim. For about 100 years this was an independent Jewish state. The Maccabean victory was attributed to their spiritual motivation and their zeal for the Torah. There were however tensions with the Pharisees and scribes giving pre-eminence to their religion whilst the Sadducees and priests formed an aristocracy more in sympathy with secular concerns.

In 67 BC a fierce contest for supremacy broke out between two Hasmonean brothers, Aristobulus and the high priest Hyrcanus II. The Romans had by then established themselves in Asia and both sons tried to enlist their support with presents and promises. In 63 BC appeals were made at Damascus to the Roman general Pompey to resolve the dispute. Pompey was, according to the historian Sallust, 'honest in face, shameless in heart' and his sadism and greed in former battles earned him the name, 'the young butcher' (Montefiore, 2011: p.71). He promptly marched on to Jerusalem, arrested Aristobulus and laid siege to the Temple Mount. He attacked on a Sabbath and feast day cutting the throats of the priests protecting the altar. Judaea became a Roman protectorate. Pompey returned to Rome in triumph. Aristobulus was exiled and Hyrcanus II was left to rule as high priest and "ethnarch", ruler of the nation, a lesser title than king. For twenty-three years Hyrcanus II ruled Judaea autonomously. He was obliged to pay tribute to Rome and support Roman policies and military actions in the Eastern Mediterranean. Provided he maintained law and order, Rome was not interested in the internal affairs of Judaea but would provide support to protect him and maintain him in office should he be threatened.

The Herods

Hyrcanus appointed his friend and supporter, Antipater, as military governor. Antipater was the first of the Herods. He was not a Jew by birth but an Idumaean or Edomite, coming from the area south of Judaea. They were tough pagan warriors, described by historians at the time as a most barbarous and bloody nation. They had recently been converted en masse to Judaism. Antipater had embraced the Jewish religion and brought up his children as Jews.

In Italy, Julius Caesar crossed the Rubicon in 49 BC, and about eighteen months later defeated Pompey's troops. Pompey fled to Egypt but Julius Caesar pursued him. When he arrived, the Egyptians presented him with the pickled head of Pompey as a welcoming gift. Egypt was a divided country ruled by King Ptolemy XIII but with the deposed queen Cleopatra anxious to regain her power. Cleopatra demanded a private audience with Julius Caesar, master of the Roman Empire. According to legend she made a theatrical entrance by being carried in wrapped in a carpet. Cleopatra was twenty-one:

'Her sex appeal, together with the charm of her conversation, and the charisma evident in everything she said or did, made her, quite simply, irresistible,' wrote Plutarch (Holland, 2004, p.328).

She fascinated the battle-worn, fifty-two year old Julius Caesar. They had an affair and she bore a son. In the complex world of sex and politics, Cleopatra needed the support of Rome whilst Julius Caesar saw the prospect of adding Egypt to the Roman Empire. Caesar was committed to Cleopatra's cause. The Egyptians rose up against them and they found themselves trapped in Alexandria. Antipater, then military governor of Palestine, saw the opportunity to gain favour from Julius Caesar. With a force of three thousand men he went to Alexandria and with the assistance of Jews living in Egypt, helped Julius Caesar restore the throne to Cleopatra. Antipater's family, best known as the Herods, were subsequently always treated favourably by the Romans.

Two of Antipater's sons, Phasael (or Faisal as his mother was an Arab) and Herod, later to be known as Herod the Great, were made governors of Judaea and Galilee respectively. Herod immediately began to establish his reputation. He was only fifteen years old when there was an insurrection led by Ezekias the Galilean. Herod summarily executed him 'as well as a great number of robbers that were with him' (Josephus, *Antiquities* 14:9.2). The Jewish court, the Sanhedrin, summoned Herod for trial as this was unlawful. Realising what an important ally Antipater and his sons were in maintaining law and order in Palestine, the Roman governor of Syria ordered Herod's acquittal and gave him greater powers.

Aristobulus, then in exile, and his son Antigonus, still had ambitions to rule Judaea. Aristobulus was assassinated by friends of Pompey but Antigonus sought the support of the Parthians, who at that time were the principal military threat to Rome. In 40 BC the Parthians successfully invaded Syria and Palestine. Antigonus was made king of Judaea. Hyrcanus II and Phasael were captured. Hyrcanus II was permanently disqualified from his role as high priest by the simple expedient of cutting off his ears. According to Levitical law no one with a physical imperfection could enter the inner temple. Herod had managed to flee to Rome.

Rome, as an imperial power, would not wish to see a chosen and loyal ruler such as Hyrcanus II overthrown by force. Herod was the obvious choice as a sanctioned replacement: he was a strong man and an excellent soldier, with staunch loyalties to Rome. His father had been an effective military governor but had died of poisoning by an Israeli. The Roman senate, at the instigation of Mark Anthony, appointed Herod the Great as king of Palestine. He was given the support of Roman troops but it was three years before they could drive the Parthians out of Jerusalem (36 BC). Herod signalled his triumph by massacring almost all of the Sanhedrin, as they had supported his rival Antigonus. Mark Anthony personally beheaded Antigonus.

Herod was gifted with infinite energy and adroitness. He has been compared with Solomon for his taste for magnificence and women. He had ten wives. It was no mean feat to bring the state safely through the trauma of the Roman civil wars that culminated when Octavian (Augustus) defeated Anthony and Cleopatra at the naval battle of Actium in 31 BC. Herod cultivated strong relationships first with Anthony and then with Augustus. With control of the whole of Palestine and Roman patronage, he could play the role of a great king. Provided the country was stable, taxes were collected and the interests of Rome were not threatened in any way, Rome was content to delegate responsibility. In Herod's time, Palestine was not an occupied country under Roman military rule. It was very largely an independent state, although Roman soldiers were garrisoned there and could be called to support Herod should the need arise. This was one of the few countries in the Roman Empire that was not obliged to give sacrifices in honour of Caesar.

Herod had a vast building programme. On the county's west Mediterranean coast he built a large city with a magnificent protected harbour, Caesarea, and placed a temple dedicated to Rome and Augustus on a centrally located hill. On the other hand, to court the favour of the Jews, he rebuilt the Temple in Jerusalem, whose grandeur was only exceeded by his palaces in Caesarea and Jerusalem. Josephus wrote:

> The sanctuary had everything that could amaze either mind or eye. Overlaid all round with stout plates of gold, in the first rays of the sun it reflected so fierce a blaze of fire that those who endeavoured to look at it were forced to turn away as if they had looked straight at the sun (Josephus, *The Jewish War,* 5:5.6).

Jerusalem became one of the greatest cities of the eastern world.

Herod married Mariamme, a Hasmonean princess, as her family still commanded the loyalty of much of the populace. Perhaps Herod thought that such a marriage would result in reconciliation between the two groups. What happened was a bitter battle for power between Herod and Mariamme's family, especially her mother. Nevertheless, the Jews hated Herod as he imposed oppressive taxes to pay for the new buildings and kept order by a reign of terror, crucifying or burning offenders. More particularly his Hellenising influences offended many Jews. His ministers were Greek, he built Greek temples in the cities of Palestine, and introduced Greek and Roman games to Jerusalem. Josephus recorded that Herod erected a large golden eagle, an emblem of Roman power, over the great gate of the Temple.

> Two of the most eloquent men among the Jews [Judas and Matthias], and most celebrated interpreters of the Jewish laws, persuaded their students to scale the Temple in broad daylight (Josephus, *Antiquities,* 17:2.4).

They pulled down the eagle and destroyed it with axes. Judas, Matthias and forty young men were arrested. Herod had them burnt alive.

Towards the end of his life he became more vengeful, killing his wife Mariamme, her brother, her grandfather and three of his sons. Mariamme was suspected to have been unfaithful, the others were charged with treason. His ruthless paranoia has been compared to that of Joseph Stalin or Idi Amin. Nevertheless, he prevented the return of the civil war that had marred the Hasmonean period. Augustus, who had approved the trial of his first two sons, remarked that he would rather be Herod's pig than his son (quoted. in Sanders, 1995 p. 19).

Herod died in 4 BC after ruling for thirty-three years. His death was agonising. Probably as a result of heart and kidney failure his lower body became grossly swollen with suppurating sores. He was buried at Herodium, a towering desert fortress he had built for that purpose a day's march south of Jerusalem. It was a lavish occasion. Josephus wrote:

> The bier was of solid gold, studded with precious stones, and had a covering of purple, embroidered with various colours. On this lay the body enveloped in purple robe, a diadem

encircling the head and surmounted by a crown of gold, the sceptre beside his right hand (Josephus, *Antiquities,* 17:7.3).

In the very last days of his life, he altered his will twice. His last decision was to divide his kingdom into three provinces, each administered by one of his sons, Herod Antipas, Herod Phillip II and Herod Archelaus. This was later ratified by Augustus, but he withheld the title of king, giving the lesser titles of ethnarch or tetrarch.

Herod Antipas was made tetrarch of Galilee and Perea (part of today's Jordan). This was a rich and fertile part of Palestine. The northern part was mountainous and the southern part rolling hills. Josephus wrote:

Their soil is universally rich and fruitful, and full of plantations of trees of all sorts, insomuch as it invited the most slothful to take pains in its cultivation, by its fruitfulness (Josephus, *The Jewish War* 3; 3.2).

Olive oil was a major export commodity. The Sea of Galilee provided a flourishing fishing industry with towns along its shoreline such as Capernaum. Food was exported to the then almost barren Judaea with its much harsher climate and little rain.

Herod Antipas ruled Galilee and Perea on the same understanding with Rome that his father had ruled Palestine. He paid tribute, co-operated with Rome, and maintained law and order. In return he had the freedom to rule as he wished. He did not interfere with Jewish practices, maintaining Jewish law, Jewish schools and synagogues. He minted his own coins, an indication of his degree of independence from Rome. He was influenced by Greek culture and decorated his palace with pictures of animals, which many regarded as graven images. Like his father, he undertook major construction work. First he rebuilt the capital of Galilee, Sepphoris, which had been destroyed in the insurrections of 4 BC and 6 AD. Sepphoris lies about four miles north of Nazareth. Later he built a new capital on the shores of Lake Galilee which he named after the then emperor, Tiberias. This did not gain favour with the Jews, it had been a burial place and to live in such a location rendered Jews unclean. Many of the inhabitants were either forced or bribed to live there.

To fund his building work, Antipas and the small governing class would, through taxation, take between 50 and 65% of the total national income. This resulted in gross inequality. The merchant classes could make a good living but the large peasant class would live at or close to subsistence level. Agrarian societies produced more people than the dominant classes found it profitable to employ. This created an expendable class that would include petty criminals, beggars and under-employed itinerant workers. Galilee was a green and pleasant land with considerable resources but it was marked by extreme social inequality.

Antipas' marriage to his half-brother's wife Herodias was criticised by John the Baptist but this will be discussed later. In 39 AD Herodias thought that her husband, who had ruled for forty-three years as tetrach (ruler of a fourth), should be elevated to king. They went to Rome but the emperor Gaius Caligula had received evidence that Antipas 'had armour sufficient for 70,000 men ready in his armoury' and that he had been plotting against Tiberias and Gaius (Josephus, *Antiquities* 18: 7.2). Antipas and Herodias were exiled to Lyon in Gaul.

Herod Phillip II was appointed tetrarch to the area to the northeast of Galilee, comprising Iturea, Batanea and Trachonitis (Luke 3:1). He married Salome, the daughter of Herodias, and ruled from 4 BC to 34 AD. He showed moderation, justice and good government.

Herod Archelaus was appointed ethnarch of Samaria, Judaea (including Jerusalem) and Idumaea and reigned 4 BC to 6 AD. His was not going to be an easy task as there were hostilities between the Jews and the Samaritans. The vast crowds that attended religious festivals in Jerusalem were always a potential source of disruption. At the first Passover festival after the death of Herod the Great, the pilgrims ran amok, believing his death was a sign of deliverance. They stoned Archelaus' guards but he responded by sending in the cavalry and slaughtering three thousand people in the Temple. He then departed to Rome to confirm his appointment. In the meantime, Sabinus, Rome's representative, ransacked the palace to find his fortune. Further riots ensued. Josephus, critical of their actions wrote, 'The nation was infected with this doctrine to an incredible degree'. He describes 'very great robberies and murders of our principal men' and 'the taking and demolishing of cities' (Josephus, *Antiquities* 18:1.1 and 6). Herod Archelaus appears to have lacked the skill to balance the art of compromise with the need to suppress dissent. Consequently, he ruled ruthlessly and with great cruelty. One of the main instigators was Judas, a Galilean. He was the son of Ezekias, who had previously caused unrest in Galilee and had been summarily executed by Herod. Judas raided the arsenal in Sepphoris, the capital of Galilee, and created chaos in the region.

Varus, the Roman governor of Syria, intervened and with his three legions restored order. In the process, he burnt the city of Sepphoris and took the inhabitants as slaves. In Samaria he destroyed the villages and 'all places were full of fire and slaughter'. In Jerusalem he crucified two thousand of the leading rebels. Judas escaped with a Pharisee called Zadok and formed a rebellious association known as the Zealots. They forbade Jews to pay taxes to Caesar or acknowledge any god but theirs. Joseph and Mary, on their return from Egypt to Galilee, are said to have avoided this area (Matt. 2.22).

Herod Archelaus' behaviour was unacceptable even to the Romans and Augustus removed him. The area, once again, became a Roman province. One incident is worthy of comment. In 6 AD, as a consequence of Herod Archelaus' misrule, Augustus sent a Roman senator, Quirinius, to Judaea to undertake a census and enforce a new tax regime.

Administration of Judaea was assigned to a Roman official from the lower aristocracy with the title "prefect" or "procurator". He lived in one of Herod the Great's luxurious palaces at Caesarea on the Mediterranean coast. At his disposal there would be about three thousand soldiers. Scattered around the region there were small garrisons, one being stationed in the Antonia Fortress next to the Temple in Jerusalem. The prefect was subordinate to the legate of Syria, who had considerable forces at his disposal. If the need arose these troops could be called upon in Judaea. The Roman prefect and additional troops came to Jerusalem during the major festivals to ensure that the huge crowds did not get out of hand. The prefect's prime responsibility was to maintain law and order. To this end he had the power to execute anyone he considered a threat to Roman interests. This included Roman citizens and soldiers. He did not have to formulate a charge that would stand up in a court in Rome. Most prefects exercised their power with discretion, as unduly arbitrary and harsh action could result in rebellion with further problems. On the other hand, the citizens could make representations to the Syrian legate or possibly to Rome with a view to having them removed.

Local government was left in the hands of the elders, usually priests, of the towns and villages. The situation in Jerusalem was more complicated. The high priest governed Jerusalem. He was supported by an inner circle of advisors and a governing council, the Sanhedrin. The constitution and power of the Sanhedrin remains a subject of controversy. The high priest was ultimately responsible for the Temple guards who policed the city. They amounted to several thousand, but were probably not full-time, instead serving on a rotational basis. He had full judicial powers. Rome had allowed notices to be placed in the Temple forbidding any Gentile to proceed beyond a certain point. If they transgressed then anyone, even a Roman soldier, could be summarily executed. The high priest and his council had to organise the collection and payment of tribute.

The Jewish high priests were hereditary appointments. The first priest was Aaron, Moses' brother. It was almost four hundred years later, c. 970 BC, that Zadok the priest anointed Solomon king (1 Kings 1.28–45). Subsequent high priests were thought to be descendants of Zadok. During the Persian and Hellenistic periods of domination the high priests were the leaders of the nation. When the Hasmoneans gained power, the Zadokite family was deposed and Simon became high priest (1 Macc. 14.41–49JB). When Herod became king he had no claim to be high priest as his ancestry was largely Idumean rather than

Jewish. He simply appointed the high priest. The Romans continued the tradition but chose those with aristocratic priestly backgrounds. This arrangement suited the Romans. This was the traditional form of government and the Jews respected the high priest although perhaps not to the same extent as before they were political appointments. If people wanted to deal with Rome they went through the high priest. If Rome wanted to communicate with the people, the prefect summoned the high priest. If things went wrong then the high priest was held accountable.

The high priest at the time of Jesus was Joseph Caiaphas. He was a success. He served seventeen years, longer than any other high priest under Roman rule. For ten of those years (26–36 AD) Pontius Pilate was prefect and was at times insensitive to Jewish religious feeling. One night his soldiers took ensigns bearing Caesar's effigy into Jerusalem. It was contrary to Roman custom to use Caesar's effigy in such circumstances and highly offensive to the Jews. A large crowd went to Caesar's headquarters in Caesarea and appealed for their removal. On the sixth day Pilate surrounded them with his soldiers and threatened them with immediate death if they did not end their demonstration. The Jews immediately lay on the ground and exposed their necks preferring instant death 'rather than the wisdom of their laws be transgressed'. Pilate relented, perhaps out of concern for possible repercussions (Josephus, *Wars* 2:9.4;*Antiquities* 18:3.2).

On another occasion, a large demonstration occurred when Pilate sought to appropriate Temple funds to the building of a new aqueduct to Jerusalem. Roman soldiers, disguised as ordinary people but with hidden daggers, infiltrated the crowd and at a given signal they:

> ... laid upon them much greater blows than Pilate had commanded of them... there were a great number of them slain by this means, and others of them ran away wounded; and thus an end was put to this sedition (Josephus, *Wars, 2:9.4; Antiquities, 18:3.2).

Philo, a highly respected Jew who lived in Alexandria, describes Pilate as a man of 'inflexible, stubborn and cruel disposition' whose administration was marked by his 'veniality, thefts, assaults, abusive behaviour and his frequent murders of untried prisoners' (quoted. in Fredriksen, 2000, p.171). The second-century Roman historian Tacitus, himself no Judeophile, implicitly acknowledges the misgovernment of Judaea.

Herod Agrippa, grandson of Herod the Great, was brought up in Rome. His best friend was Emperor Tiberias' son. Their lives were dominated by high living and debauchery. Later he became friendly with Caligula, who enjoyed a similar lifestyle. When Herod Phillip II died in 37 AD, Caligula appointed Herod Agrippa tetrarch of Iturea, Trachonitis and Bantanea. Herod Agrippa spread the allegation that Herod Antipas was plotting against Caligula resulting in Antipas' forced exile to Lyon in Gaul. Agrippa was then given responsibility for Galilee and Perea. His policy was to please the Pharisees without offending the Romans. He scarcely visited his lands, preferring the company of Caligula and the pleasures of Rome. Caligula became increasingly egotistic and decreed that his own image be worshipped across the empire, including the Holy of Holies in the Temple. Riots erupted in protest even in Alexandria and the governor of Syria was ordered to enforce the decree. Agrippa was in Rome at the time and as a result of his brave intervention Caligula rescinded the order. He regarded the early Christians as schismatic and persecuted them:

> About that time Herod [Agrippa] the king laid violent hands upon some who belonged to the church. He killed James the brother of John with the sword; and when he saw that it pleased the Jews, he proceeded to arrest Peter also. This was during the days of Unleavened Bread (Acts 12.1–3).

According to Acts, Peter survived by the intervention of an angel. Later, Agrippa was holding court in Caesarea dressed in his gold-encrusted robes when he was taken ill with stomach pains, 'was eaten by worms' and died (Acts 12.23). His son was too young to rule and Palestine was ruled by a succession of procurators subordinate to the governor of Syria. The procurators generated dissatisfaction and hatred amongst the Jews by their oppression and extortion as will be explored in the next section.

The Destruction of Jerusalem

In Samaria c. 48 AD large crowds gathered around a prophet called Theudas. It was anticipated that he would part the waters of the river Jordan and march on Jerusalem as a reenactment of the acts of Joshua. Roman cavalry attacked them, killing many. They also took Theudas alive, beheaded him and carried his head to Jerusalem. A few years later, the two sons of Judas the Galilean, James and Simon, were crucified like their father for instigating rebellion (Josephus *Antiquities* 20:5.2).

Under Cumanus (48–52 AD), there were large crowds in Jerusalem for the Passover and armed soldiers were positioned within the Temple cloisters as security. Josephus describes how 'A certain soldier let down his breeches and exposed his privy members to the multitude, which put those that saw him in a furious rage'. Soldiers in full armour were sent as reinforcements. Josephus records that no fewer than 20,000 died, many crushed in the narrow streets as they tried to escape (Josephus, *Antiquities* 20:5.3).

The insurrections continued with fighting between Galileans and Samaritans and more crucifixions. The situation deteriorated under the notorious mismanagement of Antonius Felix (52–60AD). Tacitus described Felix as one who 'practised every kind of cruelty and lust, wielding the power of a king with the instincts of a slave' (quoted in Montefiore p. 116). A Jew from Egypt proclaimed that he was a prophet and would march on Jerusalem to bring down its walls (Josephus, *Wars* 2:13.5). A large crowd gathered. According to Luke they numbered four thousand (Acts 21.38). Felix attacked and scattered the crowd.

The Zealots increased in number and daring. Large-scale fighting commenced in Caesarea. The governor of Syria subdued Galilee but was unable to take Jerusalem and was forced to retreat. About five thousand Roman soldiers were killed and the eagle of the legion captured. Roman pride had to be avenged.

In the meantime various Jewish factions fought for control of Jerusalem. First there were gangs of young brash brigands who attacked the Temple priests. With the city in disarray, John of Giscala saw his opportunity. With his Galilean fighters and Idumean supporters he rampaged through the streets killing twelve thousand, so that the Temple overflowed with blood. They killed the high priest, Ananus, and other priests, stripped them and stamped on their naked bodies before throwing them over the walls to be eaten by dogs. The Idumeans departed with their booty leaving John of Giscala to dominate the city. Inhabitants of Jerusalem asked another young warlord, Simon ben Giora, to rid them of the tyrant. Fierce fighting ensued.

Rome now sent their most experienced general, Vespasian, with a large force. In the summer of 67 AD he brought the country districts into subjection. He made no attempt to take Jerusalem as those inside the city were making his ultimate objective easier. There were internal feuds, murder, disease, famine and panic. In 69 AD Vespasian was proclaimed emperor of Rome and his son Titus took over the conduct of the war. The following year, after a three-month siege, Jerusalem fell. Most of the inhabitants were massacred; those who survived were sold into slavery or reserved for Titus' triumphal march in Rome. This was the most extravagant triumphal procession in Rome's history. Floats up to four stories high depicted the battle. Floats exhibited the captured wealth of Jerusalem including the splendours of the Temple, the golden table, the candelabra and the Law of the Jews. The riches of Jerusalem funded the building of the Colosseum in Rome. Simon ben Giora was paraded with a noose around his neck. He and other rebel leaders were executed to the delight of the crowds outside the Temple of Jupiter.

A few fortresses held out, most notably Masada, built by Herod the Great, on an almost inaccessible mountaintop overlooking the Dead Sea. After a three-year siege all the inhabitants committed suicide.

Palestine became a colony under a Roman governor. The Jews had no political rights, no Sanhedrin, no Temple, and were banned from visiting the Temple Mount. Their Temple tax was replaced by *Fiscus Judaicus* to raise money to rebuild the Temple of Jupiter. The Jews were utterly humiliated.

In 130 AD, the emperor Hadrian, famous for his defensive wall between Scotland and England, visited the wrecked city of Jerusalem. He embarked on building a classical Roman town based on the worship of Roman, Greek and Egyptian gods. All trace of its Jewish history was destroyed. Amongst other buildings he created a Temple of Jupiter with a statue of Aphrodite outside it. He planned a shrine on the Temple Mount with a huge equestrian statue of himself. He erected nude statues of his true love, the Greek boy Antinous. Hadrian was bisexual. Jerusalem was renamed Aelia Capitolina. Aelia in honour of Hadrian, his full title being Publius Aelius Hadrianus, and Capitolinus after the god most associated with the Roman Empire, Jupiter Capitolinus. Hadrian deliberately renamed Judaea Palistina after the Jews' ancient enemies the Philistines. Hadrian accepted the conventional Roman view that the Jews were demented fanatics. Tacitus had described the Jews as 'sinister and revolting' bigots, with bizarre superstitions including monotheism and circumcision, who despised Roman gods, 'rejected patriotism' and have 'entrenched themselves by their very wickedness' (quoted. in Montefiore 2011 p. 131).

A revolt was mounted between 132 and 135 AD by Simon bar Kokhba, whom many Jews considered to be the new David or even the Messiah. He defeated the Roman governor and his two legions. Hadrian returned with his best commander, Julius Severus. Their revenge was ruthless. Cassius Dio recorded the events at the time. He wrote, 'Very few survived. Fifty of their outposts and 985 villages razed to the ground. 585,000 were killed in battles' and many more by 'starvation, disease and fire'. Hadrian not only enforced the ban on circumcision but banned the Jews from even approaching Aelia Capitolina. Jerusalem was no longer the focus for Judaism. It was in this tumultuous atmosphere that Christianity was born.

II

Religious Practice in Palestine at the time of Jesus

The basis of Judaism is a collection of books, or more correctly scrolls, that date from 1,000 to 150 BC and had been amalgamated and revised over the centuries to create the Hebrew Scriptures. The underlying theme of these texts is that there is only one God and there is none beside him. He created the universe and is characterised as showing mercy, kindness and justice. He made man in his own image and expects him to show the same attributes and to act according to the revealed ethical and spiritual responsibilities. The relationship between God and man is fundamentally a moral one. The scrolls that form the Hebrew Scriptures have been assembled into three categories. These are known as the Torah or Pentateuch, Nevi'im or the Prophets and the Ketuvim or the writings; hence the acronym, TaNaKh. This chapter offers a very brief summary of religious practice at the time of Jesus, intended to assist in our understanding of the New Testament within the context of its original roots

The Torah or Pentateuch

The Torah, meaning "law" or "instruction", comprises five books. Genesis, as its name implies, covers the beginning of the universe and the human race. Exodus describes the deliverance of the Israelites from Egypt by Moses and their period in the Sinai desert and the giving of the law and commandments on two tablets of stone (Exod. 34.8). Further details of the moral, ceremonial and civil laws constitute the book of Leviticus. The books of Numbers and Deuteronomy covers the forty years of wandering in the desert until the tribes of Israel reach the plains of Moab in sight of the promised land of Canaan. The Torah is the most revered section of the Hebrew Bible.

Nevi'im or The Prophets

These include Isaiah, Jeremiah and Ezekiel. It is generally accepted that Isaiah is an anthology comprising three authors, representing chapters 1 to 39, chapters 40 to 55 and chapters 56 to 66 respectively. It was the prophets (literal meaning "one who has been called") who interpreted the political events in a religious context. They believed that their history was an account of God's direct intervention in their history. The prophets are recorded as working miracles, healing the sick and foretelling the future, but their main role was to highlight the shortcomings of the Israelites and their lapses from the Torah. God's selection of Israel, they argued, did not mean privilege, but responsibility. If the nation neglected that responsibility, it would be punished:

You [people of Israel] only have I known [or acknowledged] of the families of the earth; therefore I will punish you for all your iniquities (Amos 3.2).

Sons have I [God] reared and brought up, but they have rebelled against me. The ox knows its owner, and the ass its master's crib; but Israel does not know, my people does not understand (Isaiah 1.2–3).

The prophets argued that this was punishment and not rejection. God will not break his covenant with Israel. He will redeem them provided they repent and return to the Torah. The prophets use analogies to emphasise God's constancy and consolation in Israel's suffering. 'God is like a father and Israel, his son' (Hos. 11.1–3). 'God is Israel's shepherd who has allowed his flock to scatter but will gather them in again' (Jer.

31.10–11). 'Israel is like an unbroken calf that protests at the yoke but God will train her' (Jer. 31.18–19).

They all interpret Israel's disastrous conflicts with the Assyrians and the Babylonians as divine judgement and a call for repentance. This is tempered with a message of hope. The prophets believed that God, having created heaven and earth, would at some time establish his divine kingdom on earth. In Deutero-Isaiah we have a vision of the heathen acknowledging the God of Israel:

> Thus says the Lord: 'The wealth of Egypt and the merchandise of Ethiopia, and the Sabeans, men of stature, shall come over to you and be yours, they shall follow you; they shall come over in chains and bow down to you. They will make supplication to you saying: God is with you only, and there is no other, no god besides him' (Isaiah 45.14).

Consequently, they would submit to the Israelites.

> With their faces to the ground they shall bow down to you, and lick the dust of your feet. Then you will know that I am the Lord; those who wait for me shall not be put to shame (Isaiah 49.23).

The nations are then pictured bringing their riches for the service of the Temple. The Bedouin tribes send camels, people from Sheba (south-western Arabia) bring gold and frankincense, Arabian nomads bring sheep to be sacrificed, precious woods come from Lebanon's forests and from the west come innumerable ships laden with treasure (Isaiah 60.1–14).

Israel's suffering has a redemptive meaning. Through chastisement, Israel will repent and act with justice and righteousness. Israel's faithfulness to the Torah will bring peace to the whole world.

> From out of Zion shall go forth the law [Torah] and the word of the Lord from Jerusalem... nation shall not lift

sword against nation, neither shall they learn war any more (Isaiah 2.3–4).

There is a message of hope and expectation.

There shall come forth a shoot from the stump of Jesse [i.e. a second David] and a branch shall grow out of his roots… And his delight shall be in the fear of the Lord (Isaiah 11.1-3).

Contrary to the belief of many Christians, Judaism does not reflect a struggle to comply with complicated rules and regulations. Rather it is a desire that one's life should reflect the Torah and the freedom this brings. It is a paradox that to live with a set of rules or beliefs is to many people a liberating experience. Jeremiah, whilst in exile in Babylon, expressed this fluently when he wrote:

I [Jehovah] will put my law within them, and I will write it upon their hearts; and I will be their God, and they shall be my people. And no longer shall each man teach his neighbour and each his brother, saying, "Know the Lord" for they shall know me, from the least of them to the greatest, says the Lord; for I will forgive their iniquity, and I will remember their sin no more (Jer. 31.33–34).

There are also twelve minor prophets, so designated not because they are less important but their books are much shorter. Included are a number of books that are essentially historical but are regarded as "former prophets". These are Joshua, Judges, Samuel 1 and 2, and Kings 1 and 2.

Ketuvim or The Writings

This is a collection of sacred writings that cannot be classified as either the Torah or Nevi'im. Psalms, Proverbs and Job constitute a high point of the TaNaKh as poetic literature. A second group consist of the Song of Songs, Ruth, Lamentations,

Ecclesiastes and Esther, some of which are regarded as rather secular. Song of Songs is essentially in praise of sexual love although some interpret this as God's love of Israel. Ecclesiastes is a sceptical view of life and Esther does not mention the word God once. Finally, we have Daniel, a highly symbolic account of world history; Ezra and Nehemiah recount the return from Babylon and the rebuilding of the Temple; and Chronicles 1 and 2 largely supplement accounts of David and Solomon.

The post-exile writings differ in tone from that of the earlier prophets. Idolatry and heathen practices were no longer the cardinal sins of the people. The people are pictured as being disheartened, with an indifference to religion. The emphasis moves to reasoning, exhortation, warnings and promises. The Book of Proverbs deals with the need for discipline of thought and regulation of conduct with prominence being given to ethical rather than theological matters. Many books emphasise observance of the Torah, Temple worship and racial purity.

A dialectical element begins to appear in the later works. Job questions the belief that God invariably rewards the righteous and punishes the wicked. Jonah is an allegorical story that protests against the exclusiveness of Jewish thought. Ruth conveys a similar message. It is the romantic story of Naomi, who leaves Bethlehem at a time of famine and goes to Moab. Her two sons marry Moabite women, Orpah and Ruth. Naomi's husband and both sons die and she is destitute. She decides to return home but Ruth insists on staying with her, 'for where you go I will go, and where you lodge I will lodge; your people shall be my people, and your God my God' (Ruth 1.16).

Ecclesiastes was written about 200 BC and probably reflects the beginning of Greek cultural influence on Jewish thought. For the individual and the race alike, existence is a meaningless, barren cycle in which effort is unavailing. It is futile to say that piety is rewarded with success. All that awaits the good and evil man alike is the unrelieved gloom of Sheol, the underworld abode of the dead. There is no expectation of a Messiah, no apocalyptic golden age and no hope of resurrection. To be fair, Ecclesiastes was never included in Hebrew canon of scripture but is part of the Christian Bible. The reference is appropriate as an indication of how Greek culture was beginning to permeate Jewish thought.

To capture the mood of a nation it is probably better to study their popular songs rather than the writings of their sages. These are recorded in the Psalms, which were used regularly in the synagogues and Temple. About half of the 150 Psalms are attributed to David. Almost all Biblical scholars agree that very few if any were written by David and that they belong to the post-exile period, some possibly as late as 150 BC. Whilst there are conflicting perspectives the general tone is full of faith in God's wisdom and goodness. The Psalms reiterate the concept that if the Jews were faithful to the Torah then God would reward them as had been promised in the scriptures. The converse would also apply. The reward or punishment would be experienced in this life, not in an afterlife, 'In death there is no remembrance of thee; in Sheol who can give thee praise?' (Ps. 6.5).

The Psalms are full of an expectation that God will give them victory over their enemies. They reflect one of the most notorious passages in the Old Testament, namely, the account of Israel's conquest of Canaan as recorded in Joshua chapters 6–11. In this "holy war", God commands the Israelites to kill the indigenous population including all men, women and children. Perhaps it is no surprise to read, 'Break thou the arm of the wicked and evildoer; seek out wickedness till thou find none. The Lord is king forever and ever; the nations shall perish from his land' (Ps. 10.15–16). More poignantly, 'Happy shall he be who takes your [enemies'] little ones and dashes them against the rock' (Ps. 137.9).

There is a sense of imminence, 'Thou wilt arise and have pity on Zion; it is the time to favour her; the appointed time has come' (Ps.102.13). How this would occur is speculative. Psalms 2 and 72 refer to a righteous earthly ruler. Psalm 110 describes the ruler being both high priest and governor.

From Oral Tradition to Scrolls

The Torah became the most sacred of the texts. However, the traditions had been handed down over centuries by word of mouth. During the eighth century BC there was a literacy revolution throughout the Middle East. In Greece, the epics of Homer were committed to writing. Jewish scholars began to combine the oral accounts to compose national sagas. Those living in the southern province of Judah called their God "Yahweh", producing the so-called "J" (Jahwist or Yahwist) source of the Torah. The northern Israeli tribes called their God by a more formal title, "Elohim", the Eloist source often referred to simply as "E". They had very different views of God. J uses anthropomorphic language whereby Yahweh strolls in the Garden of Eden, shuts the door of Noah's ark, gets angry and changes his mind. In the E version, God is described in more transcendental terms. God scarcely even speaks but prefers to send an angel as his messenger. Later the Jews were to believe passionately that there was only one God, Yahweh, but neither J nor E believed this. The Jews worshiped many of the deities until the destruction of their Temple in 586 BC. Later these two accounts were amalgamated by an editor to create a single story that formed the backbone of the TaNaKh.

King Manasseh (687–642 BC), probably wishing to court favour with the dominant Assyrians, set up altars to Baal, erected an effigy of Asherah and statues of divine horses dedicated to the sun in the Temple. He also instituted child sacrifice (2 Kings 21). Josiah succeeded him and set about refurbishing the Temple. During the process the high priest, Hilkiah, "discovered" the scroll of the law which Yahweh had given to Moses on Mount Sinai (2 Kings 22.8–10). It is inconceivable that a scroll should disappear for six hundred years or had ever existed. The only rational explanation is that the priests serving in the Temple during Manasseh's reign, disapproving of the changes, had revised the Torah and added to it to endorse their proposals. They believed that this is what Moses would have said to Josiah had he been alive at the time. Josiah enacted the "second law" of Moses. This was a major reformation. To ensure purity of worship, pre-eminence is to be given to the Temple (Deut. 12.5–6). A secular judiciary independent of the Temple was advocated. The king was subject to the Torah as were his subjects. They placed a lot of emphasis on social justice. They also composed the books of Samuel and Kings, largely recounting the history of the two kingdoms, Israel and Judaea. They argued that the Davidic monarchs were the only legitimate rulers of the whole of Israel.

The Language of The TaNaKh

The TaNaKh or Jewish Scriptures were written in Hebrew, which was also the language of the liturgy and of the law. The spoken language was Aramaic, a closely related Semitic language with the same alphabet and some common words. This was why, in the synagogue, readings were interpreted for those not familiar with Hebrew.

For centuries before Jesus, Jews had been widely dispersed around the Mediterranean, the Diaspora. A large settlement of Jews was in Alexandria in Egypt. Their number exceeded the population of Jerusalem. Alexandria was not only a major commercial city but was the international centre for learning and the arts. According to a legend, King Ptolemy Philadelphus of Egypt in the third century BC was interested in the world's religions and wished to have a copy of the Torah in his celebrated library. A delegation was sent to the high priest in Jerusalem with a request that six scholars from each of the twelve tribes of Israel be dispatched to Alexandria to translate the Jewish Scriptures into Greek. They apparently did this independently but the translations were all identical. This was interpreted as clear evidence that they were divinely inspired. From the legendary number of translators, this version became known as the Septuagint, Latin for seventy, and is usually abbreviated as LXX.

It is more probable that the desire for a Greek translation originated with the Jews in Alexandria. The sentiment of those in exile is beautifully expressed in Psalm 137:

By the waters of Babylon, there we sat down and wept, when we remembered Zion. How shall we sing the Lord's song in a foreign land?

Many Jews had forgotten their Hebrew. Reading the Hebrew texts was difficult as the vowels were omitted and consequently reading was dependent on an oral tradition handed down from teacher to pupil over countless generations. The vowels were inserted into the Hebrew text by scholars known as Massoretes, working between the sixth and tenth century AD. To the Jews there was no distinction between political, religious, social and commercial activities. They were all part of one way of life as expounded in the TaNaKh. Without access to these scriptures in a comprehensible form their distinctive way of life would disappear. Greek was the common language of the day. When Paul wrote to the Romans, it was in Greek. Even today older generations of émigré populations would lament, 'When you lose the language, you leave the faith!' There was also a need to explain and defend their faith to Greek-speaking Gentiles.

The authors of the New Testament all quote from the Greek Septuagint rather than the Hebrew text. For the next thousand years, Christians used the Septuagint as the definitive book of reference. With the notable exceptions of Origen of Alexander in the third century and Jerome, who produced the Latin version known as the Vulgate at the beginning of the fifth century, there was virtually no interest in the Hebrew text. A Greek Orthodox confession of faith written in the nineteenth century as a response to Pope Pius IX, describes the Septuagint as 'a true and perfect version' of the Hebrew text (quoted in Pelikan 2005, p. 64). This has to be questioned. Thus the Hebrew phrase "the hand of God" was translated into Greek as "the power of God" to avoid the impression that the Divine was like a human being. Some Hebrew words did not have a Greek equivalent, such as all the unclean animals listed in Leviticus. There are nuances in translation. The Greek word for "messenger" was "angelos" and the word for "wind" could also mean "spirit." Psalm 104:4 in Hebrew reads as "He makes the winds His messengers" but was translated as "He makes His angels spirits" (Pelikcan, 2005, p.59). Later we will consider examples where the translation has been misleading. Suffice to quote from Ecclesiasticus, or as it is subtitled in the Greek Bible, "The Wisdom of Jesus Ben Sirach". This was originally written in Hebrew and translated by the author's grandson in Alexandria in 132 BC. He writes in his foreword:

> You are therefore asked to read this book with good will and attention and to show indulgence in those places where, notwithstanding our efforts at interpretation, we may seem to have failed to give an adequate rendering of this or that expression; the fact is that you cannot find an equivalent for things originally written in Hebrew when you come to translate them into a foreign language; what is more, you will find on examination that the Law itself, the Prophets and other books differ considerably in translation from what appears in the original text (Ecclus. (Ben Sira) Foreword 15–26 JB).

Evidence from the Dead Sea Scrolls would suggest that the contents of the Torah and Nevi'im were established by the fourth century BC. The final selection of books to be included in the third section, the Ketuvim or Writings, was made by a group of rabbis under the leadership of Rabbi Akiba of the Jamnia academy near Haifa in about 90 or 100 AD. The canon of the TeNaKh or Hebrew Bible was thus established some sixty years after the death of Jesus.

The Temple in Jerusalem

The Temple that had been built by Solomon was destroyed by the Babylonians in 586 BC. It was rebuilt in 516 BC. Herod the Great extended and rebuilt the Temple between 19 and 9 BC. As ritual sacrifice was not interrupted during this period it continued to be regarded as the second Temple. Mount Moriah on which the Temple had been built was too small to accommodate Herod's plans. He built massive retaining walls around the mountain to increase the area available. Between the mountain and the walls he created vaulted chambers, named Solomon's stables, to provide stalls for animals. The enclosed area was roughly rectangular in shape. Archaeological studies show that the walls measured about 475 metres north to south and 300 metres east to west with a total perimeter of 1,540 metres. This created a platform of about thirty-five acres on which to build the Temple. Only part of the west wall remains today, the Wailing Wall. Herod would have used the latest technology. The Roman engineer, Vitruvius (born c. 75 BC) had designed enormous devices such as sledges, wheels, cranes and winches to transport massive stones.

Most pilgrims would enter the Temple complex through a gate in the southern wall. They are called gates but were in fact decorated archways measuring five metres wide and ten metres high. The southern gate was approached by a long flight of steps built with irregular treads and risers. Care had to be taken at each step so that no one could rush up without due respect. Once inside the vast courtyard one was surrounded by the twenty-metre high walls. During the main festivals, when many thousands would be present, Roman soldiers would patrol the parapet on top of the walls. All around the walls were cloisters that had been constructed with marble pillars and carved cedar wood ceilings. Here sacrificial animals could be bought and various currencies exchanged for bona fide silver Syrian shekels, the only money acceptable to the Temple priests. Anybody, irrespective of religion or race, could enter this part of the Temple complex, known as the Court of the Gentiles.

The Court of the Gentiles was demarcated from the rest of the Temple complex by an intricately carved stone balustrade about one and a half metres high. At regular intervals there were stone plaques written in Greek and Latin forbidding any foreigner from entering the holy place. One, still in existence reads, 'No man of another nation to enter within the fence and enclosure round the Temple. And whoever is caught will have himself to blame that his death ensues'. Holy is a term we often use loosely today. In the TaNaKh it had a specific meaning. The Jews were a "chosen nation" by God and as such were "set apart" from other nations. They were special or "holy" in contrast to the common or profane masses. Holiness was a measure of separation from the common, of being put apart for God. Speaking to Aaron, God said:

> You are to distinguish between the holy and the common, between the clean and the unclean: and you are to teach the people of Israel (Lev. 10.10).

The Temple courts were designed to reflect increasing degrees of a sense of being chosen within their community.
Beyond the balustrade Jews would walk up a flight of steps through the Beautiful Gate to the Court of the Women. This was a large area in which men and women were present. A gallery enabled the women to observe sacrifices being made. A further curved flight of steps led to the Court of the Israelites to which only men who had undergone ritual purification could enter. The impurity laws have nothing to do with morality. To take two simple examples, it is not a sin to have a sexual relationship with one's wife, nor a sin to touch the corpse of a Jew or allow his shadow to fall on you. However both actions rendered one impure for a period of time. Purification involved bathing in specially constructed pools, *mikvahs*, around the Temple. Then holy water containing the ash of a sacrificed red heifer was sprinkled over the participant (Num. 19.1–6).

The men would take their sacrificial animal into the Court of the Israelites where a low balustrade would separate them from the Court of the Priests. Within the Court of the Priests was the altar of burnt offering. It was made of unwrought stone and measured fourteen metres in length and breadth. It was seven metres high and approached by a ramp. Adjacent to it was a large brass laver which priests used to wash their hands and feet between each sacrifice. Rows of rings were set in the ground to immobilise larger animals prior to slaughter. There were racks known as shambles on which the animals could be hung to facilitate flaying them. The skins were then salted. Most animals were slaughtered at the balustrade with the owner restraining the animal whilst the priest slit its throat and collected the blood to be poured around the altar thereby symbolically giving it back to

God. God was the author of life, and the blood belonged to him alone.

> The life of the flesh is in the blood; and I have given it for you upon the altar to make atonement for your souls; for it is the blood that makes atonement, by reason of the life. Therefore I have said to the people of Israel, no person among you shall eat blood (Lev. 17.11–12).

Special channels had been built around the altar to drain the blood into the river Kidron below.

Beyond was the holy place that contained the golden altar on which incense was burnt, the table of shew bread (twelve loaves replaced each Sabbath) and the Menorah, a gold seven branched candelabrum and a symbol of Judaism in which fresh olive oil was burnt. The exterior of this sanctuary was clad in gold. Even the spikes used to prevent birds settling on it were made of gold. A highly embroidered Babylonian curtain separated the ultimate Holy of Holies. This was an empty chamber which only the high priest could enter in his special vestments and that only once a year on the Day of Atonement. The infamous emperor Caligula once attempted to put an effigy of himself in the Holy of Holies but wisely retracted.

It should be remembered how complex such a logistical exercise would have been to run the Temple, particularly during feast days when many thousands of pilgrims would attend. There were scores of chambers for administrative purposes, areas for teaching, law courts, a treasury, store rooms for vestments, wood, knifes for slaughter, musical instruments and so forth. Furthermore, it was a magnificent sight visible for miles around. Standing on top of Mount Moriah and built with white marble and covered in places with gold plates it would dazzle visitors especially when the sun was shining.

Priestly Sects Within Judaism that Emerged Under Hasmonean Rule

Religious belief and practice were not universally agreed at this time as illustrated by the existence of three main sects, Sadducees, Pharisees and Essenes. There was also a fourth sect of anti-Roman revolutionaries such as the Sicarii and Zealots that need not concern us here. From this period to the end of the first century AD, the cohesive element in Judaism was not a strict code of religious belief but rather lay in legislative and administrative institutions. These were exemplified by the roles of the Sanhedrin and the universally acknowledged cultic centre, the Temple in Jerusalem. This is not to deny the importance of religious practice such as observance of the Sabbath, Hebrew Bible reading and interpretation, but to emphasise the diversity of views within this framework.

The Sadducees

The traditional belief was that the Sadducees were direct descendants of Zadok, the high priest under Solomon. In other words it was a birth right to be a Sadducee, not something to which others could aspire. As such they represented the aristocratic, privileged, wealthy and influential stratum of society. Their main purpose was to maintain the Temple and its practices. The Temple was the centre of political and social leadership. As such their role encompassed being part of the Sanhedrin or high court, collecting taxes, organising the army and negotiating with foreign powers, especially Rome.

Their religious beliefs were essentially a fundamentalist and literal interpretation of the Torah or Pentateuch. The Sadducees believed that man had free will and was not subject to fate. They did not believe that there would be rewards or punishment after death as there was no life after death. Unlike the Pharisees, they were happy to rub shoulders with Greek culture but perhaps aristocracy conveys an innate knowledge of which side one's bread is buttered.

Their fortunes waxed and waned. The Maccabee brothers, Jonathan and Simon, successively appointed themselves high priests in the Temple thus breaking the Sadducees' traditional role. Suffice to record that between 37 BC and 66 AD there were twenty-eight high priests of whom at least twenty were probably Sadducees. With the destruction of the Temple they disappeared from history as a sect.

The Pharisees

It is not known exactly when the Pharisees originated as a cohesive sect but by the time of John Hyrcaneus' rule (135–105 BC) they were a powerful party. Membership came initially from the scribes and sages who harked back to the scribe Ezra and developed and maintained an oral tradition that they believed had originated at Mount Sinai alongside the Torah of Moses. The name Pharisee means "separatist" but whether it refers to a rejection of Greek culture or an objection to worldly ambitions of the Hasmonean dynasty is unclear. Their aim was to maintain the religious spirit in accordance with their interpretation of the Law. What is clear is that under the reign of Alexander Jannaeus (104–78 BC), who appointed himself as high priest, the conflict between the people, siding with the Pharisees, and the king, became bitter and ended in cruel carnage. Alexander ordered the crucifixion of eight hundred Pharisees and held a riotous party to celebrate the spectacle. He was succeeded by his widow, Salome Alexandra, whose brother was a leading Pharisee. Under her patronage the Pharisees gained considerable political influence, particularly in the Temple rituals and as members of the Sanhedrin.

At the heart of Pharisaic belief was the concept of one God who had chosen them as a special nation and entered a covenant with them that if they obeyed the laws given through Moses they would be blessed. Failure to comply resulted in punishment. They believed that the purity laws which applied to Temple worship should also apply to home life. It is easy to get the impression from the New Testament that the Pharisees were dogmatic and uncompromising. On the contrary, the Pharisees had a more liberal and intellectual interpretation of the Pentateuch coupled with the belief that there was an oral tradition of the Law of Moses that had been transmitted over the generations and that both had to be interpreted carefully. Rather they are best characterised as people who were constantly questioning and redefining the Law of Moses. Thus in the early part of the first century AD we have the debates between the schools of Hillel, high priest and Shammai, president of the Sanhedrin. After the destruction of the second Temple, the Pharisees changed their title to Rabbis to avoid sectarian connotations. The scholarly debate continued with the Mishnah, a Jewish scripture produced between 135 and 200 AD detailing the oral traditions of the Law of Moses. The Talmud or commentary on the Mishnah consisted of two versions, the Jerusalem Talmud in the early fifth century AD and a Babylonian version completed a century later. These texts are concerned primarily with the interpretation of Jewish law with only one brief chapter in the Mishnah on theological issues.

These comments need to be placed into the context of the time of Herod the Great. Josephus claims that there were about six thousand Pharisees at the time. He also claims that there were 20,000 priests and Levites, or lesser clergy, serving the Temple. The absolute numbers may be suspect but the proportions significant. The Temple priests constituted a large and important class in society and were the only people who could offer sacrifices. The Levites undertook tasks such as controlling the gates, cleaning the Temple, supplying firewood, singing Psalms and so forth. These were part-time roles with each being seconded to one of twenty-four divisions that was responsible for a week's duty at a time. They were all present for the major festivals. When not serving at the Temple they pursued their normal occupations, only farmers being prohibited from Temple duty. Whilst some priests were Sadducees and others Pharisees, the majority had no party affiliations.

The Essenes

This sect was described by the Roman writer Pliny the Elder (23–79 AD) and by Josephus. Interest in the Essenes was renewed by the discovery of the Dead Sea Scrolls between 1946 and 1956 in eleven caves in and around the ruins of the ancient settlement of Qumran on the north-west coast of the Dead Sea, a little south of Jericho on the West Bank. They consist of almost a thousand documents written in Hebrew, Aramaic and Greek mostly on parchment. One third covers the rules and beliefs of the Essene community and the remainder are copies of the TaNaKh and Apocryphal documents. It is believed that the Essenes hid these documents in the caves as the armies of Vespasian and Titus attacked and probably annihilated them.

The Essenes had withdrawn themselves from mainstream Jewish society in about 150–140 BC to live in an esoteric community possibly led by a Sadducee. Defection may well have been triggered by Jonathan Maccabaeus when he appointed himself as high priest thereby breaking the tradition and honour of the role. They adhered to the Jewish concept of a Covenant with God but believed that they were the last "remnant" who interpreted scriptures correctly and pledged to observe its precepts with absolute faithfulness. They were fulfilling the prophetic expectations of the salvation of the righteous in the final days. It was a community full of eschatological hope.

This does not appear as a totally homogeneous society. Some documents relate to communal living and sharing in towns. Others refer to a monastic pattern of life for celibate men in the desert. They relinquished all their belongings, undertook a three-year period of induction, were subject to a hierarchical structure of control and observed strict rules. Rather than hand washing before meals they would take a ritual bath. They didn't eat meat and condemned the Temple sacrifices of animals. The Essenes were a single religious movement with two branches (Vermes, 1994, p. 111).

The Three Pilgrimage Festivals

The origin of these festivals is described in the Torah (Lev. 23.1–44) 'Three times a year you are to celebrate a feast in my honour… You must bring the best of the first-fruits of your soil to the house of Yahweh your God'. The dates of these festivals were determined by the agricultural calendar. There was a seven-day springtime festival around the barley harvest, an early summer festival when the wheat ripens and an autumn festival of "Ingathering" when olives, grapes and other fruit were harvested. These festivals were also used to commemorate key events when God intervened in the history of the Jewish nation (Deut. 16.1–17). This combination of seasonal agricultural landmarks and remembrance of their past not only created a pattern for the year but was a powerful unifying force for a sense of special nationhood.

Feast of Passover (Pesach) and Unleavened Bread

This commemorates how the Jews left slavery behind them when they were led out of Egypt by Moses. The Egyptians had refused to let the Jews leave until God sent ten plagues upon them. The last was the death of the first born. Each Jewish household was instructed to slaughter and eat an unblemished lamb and to sprinkle its blood on the door posts. God could then pass over their houses and spare them from this plague (Exod. 12). In the Temple the lambs were slaughtered on the afternoon of the fourteenth day of the month of Nisan, corresponding to the end of March or early April in the western calendar. The Passover meal was eaten just after sunset on that day being the fifteenth Nisan. The Jewish day ends at sunset rather than at midnight.

The Passover was combined with the feast of Unleavened Bread that lasted seven or eight days. It commemorates their hasty escape from Egypt when they did not even have time to let the bread rise. The Passover festival is discussed in greater detail in chapter eight of the present work.

Feast of Weeks (Pentecost or Shavuot)

The older Wheat-Harvest festival was later mandated to be held seven weeks after the Passover, equivalent to fifty days in their lunar calendar. In the New Testament it is referred to as Pentecost, meaning fifty days. It became a celebration of the giving of the Torah to Moses on Mount Sinai (Exod. 19–20).

Feast of Booths (Tabernacles or Sukkoth)

The older Ingathering festival became a commemoration of the forty years that the Jews wandered in the desert, living in temporary shelters like tents or 'Booths' (Deut. 16.13–15). In the Second Temple period, it was an eight-day festival involving the imagery of water and light. Water was brought daily from the Pool of Siloam up to the Temple and poured over the altar. Light was provided by large lamps that were lit nightly in the Temple courtyards.

At the heart of Jewish belief was the Torah. Yahweh had given precise instructions, as delivered by Moses, about how to obey him. The Torah covered all aspects of life so there was no distinction between the religious and the secular. As a result the Jews remained a cohesive and exclusive community encompassing the Diaspora of five to six million Jews living in the cities of the Roman Empire.

The Roman historian Tacitus (56–117 AD) was possibly influenced by Pompey's ransacking of the Temple in 63 BC. When Pompey entered the Holy of Holies, he found an empty space with none of the expected treasures. Tacitus wrote that the worship of Yahweh was:

> ...a novel form of worship, opposed to all that is practised by other men. The Egyptians worship many animals and images of monstrous form; the Jews have purely mental conceptions of Deity (O'Grady, 2012, p.114).

Yahweh was a new concept in the ancient world.

III

Introduction to The New Testament

The New Testament as we know it comprises twenty-seven books which may be grouped in four genres, Gospels, Acts of the Apostles, Epistles and Revelation. These were not the only books written about Jesus. Numerous books appeared that claimed to be written by apostles or close friends of Jesus. These included Jesus' disciple Peter, his brother Judas, Thomas and his female companion Mary Magdalene. Bart D. Ehraman has published an anthology of these manuscripts entitled *Lost Scriptures* which includes fifteen Gospels, five Acts of the Apostles, thirteen Epistles and a number of Apocalypses. There were very diverse views circulating at the time.

The issue came to a head when Marcion of Sinope (c.100–165), wrote his own gospel. He believed that Christianity was an entirely new religion and wished to sever all links with the Hebrew Scriptures. Irenaeus, bishop of Lyons (c.140–200) was appalled and compiled a list of texts that became the basis of the New Testament. Texts such as the Shepherd of Hermas were later rejected but others such as Hebrews and the Epistle of Jude incorporated. Other books remained the source of controversy. The canon of the New Testament as it appears in Christian Bibles appeared for the first time in a letter of Athanasius of Alexandria issued in 367 AD. This was ratified by Pope Damasus in 382 AD. At the Councils in Carthage in 397 and 419 AD, under the leadership of St. Augustine, other branches of Christianity accepted the canon of the New Testament.

The early church adopted the Septuagint or Greek translation of Hebrew Scriptures. The canon of Hebrew Scriptures was not agreed until 90 or 100 AD by a group of Pharisees who had escaped to Yavneh near Haifa. They did not include Tobit, Judith, the Wisdom of Solomon, Ecclesiasticus, Baruch and the books of Maccabees. This was referred to as the "Apocrypha" from the Greek word for "hidden". Not until the Council of Trent in 1546 did they become – and still are – part of the canon of the Christian Bible accepted by the Eastern Orthodox and Western Roman Catholic churches. The Protestant Churches accorded them second-class status, on the grounds that they were books which 'the church doth read for example of life and instruction of manners, but yet doth it not apply them to establish any doctrine' (Pelikan, 2005, p.71).

The duration and vigour of the debate leading to the formulation of the New Testament canon would indicate an awareness of discrepancies and contradictions between the various books. Nonetheless, they all proclaimed that Jesus was the promised Messiah and that the kingdom of God was "at hand". Jesus had become too immense a phenomenon in the hearts and minds of Christians to be tied to a single definition. Two principal factors are evident in the differing interpretations of the significance of Jesus. The first is the role of the Septuagint, the Greek translation of Hebrew Scriptures and its interpretation. The second is the changing historical context in which these books were written.

The Septuagint and Its Interpretation

The importance of the Septuagint to the writers of the New Testament is self-evident by the fact that they use about nine hundred direct quotes or allusions from it. What is relevant is how they interpreted the scriptures. Between 200 BC and 100 AD the Jews had developed a highly sophisticated art of interpreting scripture. They used ancient and revered texts to elevate the significance of contemporary persons or events as having been both divinely predestined and approved. This would reinforce the divine origin of the Septuagint by speaking directly to circumstances that the original author could not have foreseen. To take one example from Jewish literature, a famous rabbi of the first century AD, Akiba ben Joseph, interpreted the messianic prophecy, 'A star shall come forth out of Jacob' (Num. 24.17) as referring to Simon bar Kosiba or the "Son of the Star" the leader of the second Jewish war against Rome. The revolt failed.

The use of ancient texts as having prophetic meaning for a current situation was not confined to Jewish thinking. In particular the Sibylline texts were highly regarded by the Romans. The term is not a name but is the title of a prophetic office always held by a woman. The earliest description of a sibyl is given by Heraclitus, a Greek writing in the fifth century BC:

> But Sibylla with raving mouth uttering things without laughter and without charm or sight of scent, reaches to a thousand years by her voice on account of the god. (Parke, 1988, p.63)

There are records of ten sibyls all named after the shrine they inhabited and a large number of Sibylline scrolls appeared over the next few centuries. To the Romans, the most important was the Cumaean Sibyl near the Greek city of Naples whose inspiration came from the god Apollo. It was she who sold to Tarquinius Superbus, the last king of Rome, the original Sibylline scrolls in the fifth century BC. Some of these were preserved in the Capitoline temple of Rome and were highly revered. These oracles were regularly consulted by a body of ten special priests, seeking for prophetic guidance in major policy decisions. After the assassination of Caesar on the Ides of March, 44 BC, the Republic's citizens faced civil war until Octavian (Augustus) gained power. Four years later, P. Vergilius Maro – Virgil – reflected on this period.

Now comes the crowning age foretold in the Sibyl's songs:

A great new cycle, bred of time, begins again.
Now virginal Justice and the golden age returns,
Now its first-born is sent down from high heaven.
With the birth of this boy, the generation of iron will pass,

And a generation of gold will inherit all the world. (Virgil, *Eclogues* :4–9)

Some Christians, including St. Augustine, interpreted this as a prophesy of the coming of Christ and that the Sibyl had at least in part been inspired by the Holy Spirit. So the idea could gradually develop that the Sibyls had been intended by God as prophets to the Gentiles parallel to the Old Testament prophets to the Jews. As a consequence, images of Sibyls appeared in Catholic churches. Most notably, five Sibyls were painted on the Sistine Chapel ceiling by Michelangelo; the Delphic Sibyl, Lybian Sibyl, Persian Sibyl, Cumaean Sibyl and the Erythraean Sybil. Other images are in the library of Pope Julius II in the Vatican, in the pavement of the Siena Cathedral and above the altar in the Basilica of Santa Maria in Rome.

This method of interpreting ancient texts was highly revered. The technical term for this fulfilment interpretation is known as *pesher*. In the New Testament it is often highlighted by phrases such as, 'All this took place to fulfil what the Lord had spoken by the prophet'. St. Paul uses this technique extensively and it would have been a persuasive argument to his Hellenistic audiences who had a high regard for ancient texts. It is too easy to simply refer to the *pesher* as an intellectual exercise. Many early Christians faced bewilderment and fear. These texts would have presented spiritual reassurance and comfort. The *pesher* argument is used so extensively in the New Testament that it is part of normative Christian belief. Thus in Handel's *Messiah* three quarters of the text is taken from the Old Testament.

St. Augustine is credited for articulating the belief that, 'Grace, Concealed in the Old Testament, is Revealed in the New'. This became widely known by the original Latin couplet:

The New is in the Old concealed,
The Old is in the New revealed.

This confident assertion, however, presents problems in interpreting the New Testament. It is difficult to distinguish between historical events and *pesher* interpretation of scripture presented as history.

Changing Historical Context

Jesus was crucified, probably in 30 AD. The earliest written records of Christian belief are the letters of Paul (c. 50–60 AD) to the churches in Rome, Corinth, Galatia, Philippi and Thessalonica. Paul was born in Tarsus, Asia Minor and was a Greek-speaking Jew with Roman Citizenship. He had studied at the school of Gamaliel in Jerusalem. Initially, he was hostile to the "Jesus movement" but after a revelation on the road to Damascus he was convinced of the risen Christ and became an apostle to the Gentiles (Galatians 1). He had never met or seen Jesus. He maintained the source of his gospel was not from the original apostles but divine revelation (Gal. 1.11–12). Paul's contribution to Christian belief is considered in chapter eleven of the present work.

The rest of the New Testament was written after 70 AD when the Romans had invaded Jerusalem and the Temple was destroyed. Temple worship and sacrifice was no longer possible. The Jews were reviled and the New Testament emphasises that Christians are different and pose no threat to Rome.

The four gospels, Matthew, Mark, Luke and John, describe the events surrounding Jesus. The first three are called the Synoptic Gospels meaning "with the same eye". They can be laid out in three columns and compared. Most scholars believe that Mark was the earliest account being written soon after 70 AD. Textual analysis indicates that Matthew and Luke drew on material in Mark's gospel. They also used another long lost document called the Q document, an abbreviation of *quelle* meaning "source" in German. They wrote it in the late eighties. John's gospel was written later, sometime between 95 and 110 AD.

Mark is traditionally identified with John Mark, a cousin of Barnabas, the colleague of Paul. Papias writing in the early second century believed that Mark was not an eye witness of the Gospel events but derived his account from Peter to whom he was an assistant. He also believed that he wrote his gospel at the instigation of the Roman Christians. Mark's gospel was written very soon after the destruction of the Temple in 70 AD and the consequent chaos across the country. Christians were being vilified. Although couched as prophesy his account probably represents what was actually happening:

> They will deliver you up to councils and you will be beaten in synagogues; and you will stand before governors and kings for my sake (Mark 13.9).

Had Jesus actually prophesised this? There was no evidence of hostility to the Jesus movement prior to his last week in Jerusalem. A rift was beginning to appear between Judaism and Christianity.

> No one sews a piece of unshrunk cloth on an old garment; if he does, the patch tears away from it, the new from the old, and a worse tear is made. And nobody puts new wine into old wineskins; if he does, the wine will burst the skins, and the wine is lost and so are the skins; but new wine is for fresh skins (Mark 2.21–22).

Mark draws on the imagery of Daniel, 'when you see this disastrous abomination' (Mark 13.14) to explain the Temple's destruction. Did not Isaiah 56.7 prophesise that 'My house will be called a house of prayer for all peoples' not just Jews (Mark 11.17). Temple practice had fallen short of God's expectations, no wonder it had been destroyed. This is in contrast to Paul's teaching who, not surprisingly, hardly mentions the Temple as it was still functioning normally in his time. The main impression of Jesus in Mark's gospel is one who was a 'worker of mighty deeds' or miracles. Mark maintained that 'The time has come and the kingdom of God is close at hand' (Mark 1.15).

Matthew's identity is unknown was but on the basis that his gospel has the strongest Jewish characteristics it is thought that he was a Greek-speaking Jew. The recurring message he conveys is that Christianity is entirely consistent with Jewish tradition. He uses the *pesher* argument exhaustively, so that hardly any event in the life of Jesus is not accompanied with the word "to fulfil the scriptures" These are mostly direct quotes from the Septuagint but also allusions to Jewish history such as Jesus' period in Egypt or his forty days in the wilderness symbolising their forty years in the Sinai desert. Matthew reinforces his argument when Jesus says:

'Think not that I have come to abolish the law and the prophets; I have come not to abolish them but to fulfil them. For truly, I say to you, till heaven and earth pass away, not an iota, not a dot, will pass from the law until all is accomplished' (Matthew 5.17–18).

Not only should one obey the Torah but one should not even think of breaking the law. Christianity was the culmination of the law and the prophets. Matthew saw Jesus as the founder of a community within a Jewish matrix but with a new constituency.

Luke was a Gentile and companion of Paul. He was the author of the third gospel and the Acts of the Apostles. He wrote at about the same time as Matthew with a similar message and additional biographical details. The prologue is addressed to "Theophilus, your Excellency" and from this it is inferred that it was written for gentile Christians. The gospel was for everybody, Jews and gentiles, women as well as men, the poor, tax collectors, the good Samaritan, the prodigal son, a Roman centurion in Capernaum and so forth. By this time Christians were being persecuted in Rome. He was anxious to show that neither Jesus nor his followers could be accused of sedition against Rome. Immediately after Jesus dies on the cross we read, 'Now when the centurion saw what had taken place, he praised God, and said, "Certainly, this man was innocent!"' (Luke 23.47).

The identity of John remains a mystery. It is inconceivable that he was the Galilean fishermen called by Jesus and described as an 'uneducated, common' man (Acts 4.13). He would have had to live to almost one hundred and acquire a profound understanding of Hellenistic thought. The gospel of John was written between 95 and 110 AD. The emphasis in the Synoptic Gospels of Jesus teaching through parables about the kingdom of God has virtually disappeared. Also the belief that Jesus would return in the near future at the end of time was reinterpreted. Jesus had risen from the dead, judgement is working here and now, and eternal life is already in the possession of those who have faith. In John the main discourses are about the Incarnation, the nature of Christ and his relationship to God. John gives special emphasis to the Jewish religious festivals with Jesus making a pilgrimage to the Temple in Jerusalem on at least three occasions as an adult to celebrate Passover. The Synoptic Gospels record Jesus making only one visit to Jerusalem as an adult. John believed that with the destruction of the Temple, Judaism was well and truly finished. Jesus had replaced all the major functions of the Temple and it was through him Jews could encounter the divine presence.

> Jesus answered them, 'Destroy this temple and in three days I will raise it up'. The Jews then said, 'It has taken forty-six years to build this temple, and you will raise it up in three days?' But he spoke of the temple of his body. When therefore he was raised from the dead, his disciples remembered that he had said this (John 2.19–22).

> Jesus also said, 'If anyone thirst, let him come to me and drink. He who believes in me, as the scripture has said, "Out of his heart shall flow rivers of living water."' (John 7.37–38). Coupled with this is, 'I am the light of the world; he who follows me will not walk in darkness, but will have the light of life' (John 8.12). Any Jew would immediately associate these words with the Feast of Booths or Sukkoth when water was poured over the altar and large lamps lit in the Temple courtyard. Jesus was symbolically replacing this festival. The concept of Jesus as the sacrificial lamb needs no elaboration.

In summary, the New Testament is not a uniform theological statement but contains differing strands of thought. These strands reflect the individual author's interpretation of the Septuagint and in particular the use of the *pesher* argument. They also reflect the changing political and cultural environment in which they lived.

IV

The Birth of Jesus

This is the best known Biblical story re-enacted countless times every Christmas. It has a magical charm that has mesmerised generations. The nativity plays are based on the accounts given by Matthew and Luke. However, there is little in common between the two accounts. The only areas of agreement are that Jesus' parents were Joseph and Mary, Mary was a virgin and Jesus was born in Bethlehem.

Matthew's account is dependent on the *pesher* interpretation of the Septuagint. Joseph and Mary lived in Bethlehem and were engaged to be married when Mary became pregnant. Joseph considered breaking off the engagement when the angel of the Lord appeared to him and explained that she had conceived by the Holy Spirit.

All this took place to fulfil what the Lord had spoken by the prophet: 'Behold a virgin shall conceive and bear a son, and his name shall be called Emmanuel' which means, God with us (Matthew. 1.22–23; Isaiah 7.14).

Joseph accepts the explanation and takes her to his home where she gave birth to Jesus. Soon afterwards,

Wise men came from the East to Jerusalem, saying, 'Where is he who has been borne king of the Jews? For we have seen his star in the East and have come to worship him' (Matt. 2.1–2).

Herod is alarmed and consults the chief priests. They conclude that it must be Bethlehem because of Micah's prophecy 'But you, O Bethlehem Ephrathah, the least of the clans of Judah, out of you will be born for me the one who is to rule over Israel' (Micah 5.2).

Herod gives the wise men the location but tells them, 'Go and search diligently for the child, and when you have found him bring me word, that I too may come and worship him' (Matt. 2.8). The star apparently guides them to the precise place:

> And going into the house they saw the child with Mary his mother, and they fell down and worshipped him. Then, opening their treasures, they offered him gifts, gold and frankincense and myrrh (Matthew 2.11).

The gifts represented respectively, royalty, divinity and the power to heal. The wise men are warned in a dream not to return to Herod and that Joseph and his family should flee to Egypt 'for Herod is about to search for the child, to destroy him' (Matthew 2.13). By fleeing to Egypt they fulfilled the prophecy that, 'Out of Egypt have I called my son' (Matthew 2.15; Hos. 11.1; Exod. 4.22). Herod's subsequent massacre of all male children under the age of two in the Bethlehem area fulfilled what was spoken by the prophet Jeremiah:

> A voice was heard in Ramah, wailing and loud lamentation, Rachel weeping for her children; she refused to be consoled, because they were no more (Jer. 31.15).

It also reflects Pharaoh's slaughter of Hebrew boys during their period in Egypt (Exodus 1.14–2.10). Joseph is instructed in a dream to return to Israel but to avoid Judaea as Herod Archelaus was then the ruthless ruler but to go to Nazareth to fulfil the prophesy that 'He shall be called a Nazarene' (Matt. 2.23). There is however no equivalent verse in the Old Testament.

Matthew, in this account, demonstrates his brilliance in using the *pesher* explanation of scripture. The whole story has been predicted in scripture with the exception of the wise men. Even this is a construct of genius. Who better to persuade Herod of a potential threat to him? Herod would have had no qualms of massacring newborn boys if they were perceived as a threat to him. What better argument for Joseph and Mary to escape to Egypt and their subsequent return to Nazareth rather than their home in Bethlehem? Matthew reenacts many of the salient features in the birth of the Jewish nation in the birth of Jesus and his period in Egypt. Matthew probably did not know that Herod died in 4 BC but what was important to him was Jesus symbolically representing the new Israel.

Luke's Gospel begins with another miraculous birth that of John the Baptist, to a priest named Zechariah and his wife Elizabeth. 'But they had no child, because Elizabeth was barren, and both were in advanced years' (Luke 1.7). Zechariah was in the Temple burning incense when the angel Gabriel appeared to him and announced that his wife would have a son. Luke continues,

In the sixth month [of Elizabeth's pregnancy] the angel Gabriel was sent from God to a city of Galilee named Nazareth, to a virgin betrothed to a man whose name was Joseph, of the house of David; and the virgin's name was Mary... And behold, you will conceive in your womb and bear a son, and you shall call his name Jesus (Luke 1.26, 27, 31).

Mary responds, 'How can this be as I have no husband?' (Luke 1.34). Luke's account is more detailed and includes human touches such as Mary staying with Elizabeth for three months during her pregnancy (Luke 1.56). Contrary to Matthew's account, the angel appears to Mary rather than Joseph.

Luke places the birth of Jesus in a historical setting, 'In the days of Herod, king of Judea' (Luke 1.5). The Christian or Anno Domini era was invented by a monk, Dionysius Exiguus (c. 470–

544) working in Rome. He based his calculations on Jesus being thirty when he began his ministry (Luke 3.23). He stated that the 'present year' was '525 years since the incarnation of our Lord Jesus Christ' (quoted in Sanders, 1995, p. 11). This is the basis of the Gregorian or Western calendar. On this reckoning, Herod died in 4 BC. Either Dyonysius had miscalculated or Luke's historical setting for the birth of Jesus is erroneous.

Luke then adds more detail:

In those days a decree went out from Caesar Augustus that all the world should be enrolled, each to his own city. This was the first enrolment, when Quirinius was governor of Syria. And all went to be enrolled, each to his own city (Luke 2.1–2).

Luke uses the census as the reason for Joseph and Mary travelling from Nazareth to Bethlehem. The census had left an indelible mark on the Jewish people. Luke, writing in the Acts of the Apostles, says,

After him Judas the Galilean arose in the days of the census and drew away some of the people after him; he also perished, and all who followed him were scattered (Acts 5.37).

Josephus describes how Judas persuaded the people, 'that this taxation was no better than an introduction to slavery'. Josephus, critical of the action of the Jews continues, 'very great robberies and murders of our principal men... the taking and demolishing of cities' (Josephus, *Antiquities,* 18:1.1).

The Roman Empire was financed by taxation of the provinces. In 27 BC Augustus introduced a regular census on which calculations of tax could be based. It took the form of a property tax on land, houses, slaves and ships, and a head tax, which was levied on all adults between the ages of fourteen and sixty-five irrespective of income. The intention was to prevent those responsible for collecting the taxes from fleecing the local people to line their own pockets and not to exact money beyond the amount appointed.

Herod died in 4 BC, he was succeeded by Archelaus, who ruled Samaria and Judea with great cruelty and ruthlessness. His behaviour was unacceptable even to the Romans and he was removed in 6 AD. He was replaced with a Roman senator, Quirinius to 'take account of their substance' so that they would be appropriately taxed (Josephus *Antiquities* 18:1:1).This did not apply to Galilee as it was ruled by Antipas. He was an astute leader who maintained peace and paid the required taxes to Rome. Rome allowed him to rule for forty-three years and did not interfere with the internal affairs of Galilee. It is even more improbable that the Romans insisted that everyone should return to their ancestral home. How could Joseph have been expected to trace back his ancestry over forty-one generations as Luke describes? It would not have been in the interests of Rome to stir up tribal jealousies. Furthermore, the purpose of the census was to evaluate wealth and this could only be done in their place of domicile. Ten years had elapsed between the death of Herod and the census in Judea. Luke's account lacks historical credibility.

Luke describes Joseph, being of the lineage of David, taking Mary to Bethlehem to be enrolled.

> And while they were there, the time came for her to be delivered. And she gave birth to her first-born son and wrapped him in swaddling clothes and laid him in a manger, because there was no place for them in the inn (Luke 2.6–7).

After the birth of Jesus he is visited by shepherds, reflecting that David was once a shepherd. Luke records that Jesus was circumcised on the eighth day (Luke 2.21; Lev. 12.3). He was then taken to the Temple in Jerusalem 'to present him to the Lord' (Luke 2.22; Exod. 13.2) and 'to offer a sacrifice according to what is said in the law of the Lord, "a pair of turtledoves, or two young pigeons"' (Luke 2.24; Lev. 12.6–8). This would have been the offering of the poor. Luke concludes, 'And when they had performed everything, according to the law of the Lord, they returned into Galilee, to their own city, Nazareth' (Luke 2.39).

Both Matthew and Luke describe Jesus as being born of the Virgin Mary. They both rely on the *pesher* argument quoting Isaiah 7.14. The verse in the Hebrew Scriptures refers to a young woman (*almah*) but the Greek Septuagint translation refers to a virgin (*parthenas*). It is this latter version that both Matthew and Luke would have used. Isaiah's account was in response to news that Syria was on the march and was within striking distance of Jerusalem threatening the reign of Ahaz and hence the Davidic dynasty in about 700 BC. Isaiah reassures Ahaz that God will deliver them provided he has faith. Ahaz does not obediently trust God. Isaiah then predicts that a pregnant woman will shortly give birth to a son whom she will call Immanuel meaning, "God is with us" thus shaming the king's unbelief. The birth was imminent as this was a pressing emergency, not something in the distant future. Isaiah had no specific woman in mind. The child would have no special status. The significance of the story was in the naming of the child Immanuel, thus re-affirming the mother's faith. Isaiah would not have imagined God taking on a human form.

Both Matthew and Luke describe the genealogy of Jesus showing a direct lineage from David. There was a strong tradition that a Messiah would arise from the house of David. Jeremiah prophesises that:

Behold, the days are coming, says the Lord, when I will fulfil the promise that I made to the house of Israel and the house of Judah. In those days and at that time I will cause a righteous Branch to spring forth for David; and he shall execute justice and righteousness in the land (Jer. 33.14–15).

Ezekiel writes:

And I [the Lord] will set up over them one shepherd, my servant David, and he shall feed them: he shall feed them and be their shepherd. And I, the Lord will be their God, and my servant David shall be prince among them; I, the Lord, have spoken (Ezekiel 34.23–24).

The Jews were, according to Hebrew Scriptures, convinced that the Messiah would be a descendent of David.

The two genealogies differ. Joseph's father is called Jacob by Matthew and Heli by Luke. Matthew takes the lineage through Solomon but Luke traces it through Nathan. Both were sons of David. Luke may have been aware that there was a curse on Solomon's line (Jeremiah 22.30). Matthew goes back as far as Abraham. Luke takes the genealogy all the way back to Adam, the first man reflecting Paul's concept of Jesus being the second Adam (1 Cor. 15.22,45).

Nevertheless, there is a contradiction between the concept of a virgin birth and Jesus being a descendent of David through Joseph. Matthew wrote, 'Jacob the father of Joseph the husband of Mary, of whom Jesus was born, who is called Christ' (Matthew 1.16). 'Jesus, when he began his ministry, was about thirty years of age, being the son (as was supposed) of Joseph, the son of Heli' (Luke 3.23). The implication in Luke is that the supposition was wrong but there remains an inconsistency between the genealogy and the virgin birth. What is clear is that both authors trace the divine sonship of Jesus back to his birth or conception.

When we look at the Nativity story in the context of the New Testament as a whole we find different views. Mark makes no reference to the Nativity story. To him, Jesus was a Galilean, Jesus of Nazareth. According to Mark, when Jesus began to teach in a synagogue in Galilee those listening remarked 'Is not this the carpenter, the son of Mary and brother of James and Joses and Judas and Simon, and are not his sisters here with us?' (Mark 6.3).

Mark even challenges the belief that the Messiah would be a descendent of David. To quote Mark's account, and as Jesus taught in the Temple, he said:

How can the scribes say that Christ is the son of David? David himself, inspired by the Holy Spirit, declared, "The Lord said to my Lord, sit at my right hand, till I put thy enemies under thy feet". David himself calls him Lord; so how is he his son? (Mark 12.35–37).

Jesus is quoting Psalm 110 titled "A Psalm of David". Here David calls the future deliverer of his people Messiah or "Lord". The implication is that the Messiah is superior to him and therefore cannot be his son. To Mark, the decisive event in Jesus' life was not his unusual birth but his baptism. This will be discussed further in the next chapter.

Paul never mentions Mary and Joseph. All Paul tells us of the birth of Jesus was that he came from a Jewish nation, 'of their race according to the flesh is Christ' (Rom. 9:5) that he was the offspring of Abraham (Gal. 3.16) and belonged to the royal lineage of David 'according to the flesh' (Rom. 1.3) in other words by physical descent. The virgin birth does not feature in his teaching. It is not that he would have been unfamiliar with the concept of a miraculous birth. There are several birth legends in the Old Testament where women considered to be barren gave birth to sons such as the patriarchs Isaac, Jacob and Joseph and the prophet Samuel. Isaac was the first born of Sarah who was well past the menopause while her husband Abraham was a hundred. As will be discussed later, it was the resurrection of Jesus that confirmed him as the Messiah and not his life on this earth.

John's Gospel does not refer to Bethlehem nor even mention the name of Mary. The first reference to her is at a marriage at Cana in Galilee where she is simply referred to as 'the mother of Jesus' (John 2.1). John's depiction of Jesus is not dependent on Jewish history or Biblical prophecy. He implies that Jesus came from Nazareth, not the traditionally correct town of Bethlehem: 'Others said, "This is the Christ". But some said, "Is the Christ to come from Galilee?"' (John 7.41).

John uses a formula that two thousand years ago, it could be argued, would have been perceived by his audience as a much more powerful argument for the divinity of Jesus than a miraculous birth. He begins his gospel:

In the beginning was the Word, and the Word was with God, and the Word was God. He was in the beginning with God; all things were made through him, and without him was not anything made that was made (John 1.1).

In other words Jesus was "in the beginning" and his earthly point of origin is irrelevant because he comes from beyond this cosmos from his Father. This theme will be explored in chapter twelve of the present work.

It is strange how veneration of the Virgin Mary has become such a prominent aspect of Christian belief. In particular the doctrine of the perpetual virginity of Mary can only be sustained by distorting simple statements. After Jesus had taught in the synagogue in Galilee the congregation were amazed at his wisdom and questioned, 'Is not this the carpenter's son? Is not his mother called Mary? And are not his brothers James and Joseph and Simon and Judas? And are not all his sisters with us?' (Matthew 13.55–56; Mark 6.3) Maurice Wiles, Professor of Divinity at Oxford in his book *The Making of Christian Doctrine* argues that:

The worshiping instinct which was of primary influence in the earliest development of Christian doctrine was that of untutored popular devotion (Wiles, 1967, p.89).

The worship of Mary found resonance in the hearts and minds of the followers of Jesus but is not reflected by the authors of the New Testament. According to the Roman Catholic doctrine of the Bodily Assumption, Mary was sinless and consequently never experienced physical death. She was raised bodily into the presence of Christ.

It is difficult not to conclude that Matthew and Luke's accounts of the birth of Jesus are not examples of history remembered but rather of prophecy being historicised. The use of the *pesher* argument was part of the culture and a highly respected way of interpreting scripture at the time. More importantly, the Old Testament was an essential element in the Christian message. The substance of belief was not simply the facts of Jesus' life, death and resurrection, but those facts understood in the light of Old Testament Scriptures. Paul emphasises the issue when he writes:

For I delivered to you as of first importance what I also received, that Christ died for our sins in accordance with the scriptures, that he was buried, that he was raised on the third day in accordance with the scriptures (1 Cor. 15.3).

Matthew assumed that Joseph and Mary lived in Bethlehem but had to explain why they moved to Nazareth. On the other hand, Luke assumed that they lived in Nazareth but had to explain why they went to Bethlehem for the birth as foretold by scriptures. What is beyond doubt is the imagination and skill that these two authors brought to their work that the story endures to today in spite of any historical basis. The authors of the New Testament regarded their understanding of the significance of Jesus transcended biographical detail.

Was Paul, the earliest exponent of Christian belief, unwittingly closer to the historical truth? To recap he writes that Jesus came from a Jewish nation, 'of their race according to the flesh is Christ' (Rom. 9.5), that he was the 'offspring of Abraham' (Gal. 3.16) and belonged to the royal lineage of David 'according to the flesh' (Rom. 1.3), in other words by physical descent. The only authors of the New Testament to record the miraculous birth of Jesus were Matthew and Luke. They believed that Jesus was the Messiah as prophesised in the Old Testament and used this text to elaborate on details of his life. Their account of the birth of Jesus was based on the Greek Septuagint translation which referred to a baby born of a virgin rather than the Hebrew young girl. The virgin birth of Jesus remains a salient feature of Christian belief.

V

John the Baptist and Jesus

The Synoptic Gospels tell us little about Jesus until he is about thirty years of age. He seems to have followed his father's trade as a carpenter, 'Is not this the carpenter?'(Mark 6.3) He does not appear to have had any formal education. John's Gospel is quite explicit. After Jesus had taught in the temple 'The Jews marvelled at it, saying, "How is it that this man has learning and has never studied?"' (John 7.15). Matthew (13.54) and Mark (6.2) make similar comments.

Jesus' cousin, John the Baptist, began teaching and baptizing people in the river Jordan, a desert region adjacent to the Dead Sea 'in the fifteenth year of the reign of Tiberius Caesar' (Luke 3.1). This would have been 28/29 AD. According to Luke (1.5) John's father belonged to the priestly order of Abijiah. John had decided against his family's obligations to serve in the Temple and the security it would offer. Rather, he was an ascetic who 'wore a garment of camel's hair, and, a leather girdle around his waist, and his food was locusts and wild honey' (Matt. 3.4). Cloth of camel's hair was a loosely woven fabric that allowed water to permeate it readily so as to ensure total body contact with the water. His diet, available in the desert, reflected his desire for purity, endorsed in the claim that he 'came eating no bread and drinking no wine' (Matthew 11.18; Luke 7.33).

John the Baptist's message was simple, 'Repent for the kingdom of heaven is at hand' (Matthew 3.2). Repentance involved undertaking deeds of piety and justice. To the Jews these were not vague virtues but referred directly to the Ten Commandments. Piety defined one's relationship to God as in the first five commandments: worship no other gods, have no graven images and so forth. Justice meant one's relationship with others: no murder, adultery, theft, lying or coveting. Unless one repents then baptism is of no value. To those who came without evidence of repentance his words were harsh:

> You brood of vipers! Who warned you to flee from the wrath to come? Bear fruits that befit repentance... Even now the axe is laid to the root of the trees; every tree therefore that does not bear good fruit is cut down and thrown into the fire (Luke 3.7–9).

Descent from Abraham did not automatically save them from the coming judgment. Matthew characteristically focuses the condemnation on Pharisees and Sadducees (Matthew 3.7). John's use of baptism was a new ceremony adapted from the Jewish tradition of ritual bathing in the *mikva* prior to entering the Temple.

He was regarded as an extraordinary prophet with a great following as:

> ...there went out to him all the country of Judea, and all the people of Jerusalem; and they were baptized by him in the river Jordan, confessing their sins (Mark 1.5).

He follows the teaching of Amos preaching doom for a sinful nation unless they show repentance and amend their ways.

Jesus left Nazareth to join John and was baptized by him. Mark's account is straightforward:

> And when he [Jesus] came up out of the water, immediately he saw the heavens opened and the Spirit descending on him like a dove; and a voice came from heaven, 'Thou art my beloved Son; with thee I am well pleased' (Mark 1.10–11).

According to Mark this was the moment when John the Baptist realised the significance of his cousin. Other writers of the Gospels were clearly perplexed by Jesus' baptism, wondering why he needed to be baptized 'for the forgiveness of sin' (Mark1.4). According to Matthew John protested when Jesus came to be baptized, saying that Jesus should baptize him. Jesus responded, 'Let it be so now; for it is fitting for us to fulfil all righteousness' (Matt. 3.14). Luke's account is curt saying simply, 'when Jesus also had been baptized' (Luke 3.21). John's Gospel makes no mention of the baptism of Jesus. John the Baptist recognises Jesus immediately:

> And the next day he [John the Baptist] saw Jesus coming towards him and said, 'Behold the Lamb of God, who takes away the sin of the world! This is he of whom I said, After me comes a man who ranks before me, for he was before me' (John 1.29–30).

This is consistent with John's theological thesis. John the Baptist predicts the coming of the Messiah:

> For this is he who was spoken of by the prophet Isaiah when he said, 'The voice of one crying in the wilderness: Prepare the way for the Lord, make his paths straight' (Matthew 3.3).

Furthermore, 'but he who is coming after me is mightier than I' (Matthew 3.11). An alternative translation is, 'he that follows me' or my disciple. The implication being that Jesus stayed with John for some time and was at that time his right-hand man or protégé. The Synoptic Gospels give no indication that John thinks of the Messiah as a supernatural being. He is thinking of a human Messiah endowed with extraordinary power and authority similar to the judge and ruler foretold by Isaiah:

> For to us a child is born, to us a son is given; and the government will be upon his shoulder, and his name will be called Wonderful Counsellor, Mighty God, Everlasting Father, Prince of Peace (Isaiah 9.6).

Following his baptism Jesus spends forty days fasting in the desert, which in Jewish idiom just meant a long time. There he faced the three temptations. They were to transform stone into bread or provide material abundance: to do homage to Satan and be made ruler of the world, that is create a political empire: and to throw himself from the top of the temple and put himself into peril so that God could undertake a miracle (Matthew 4.1–11; Luke 4.1–12). Today we probably would not describe this experience as a series of temptations but rather as a soul-searching exercise asking the fundamental questions about one's life. Who am I? What is my purpose? What do I wish to achieve? Jesus rejects wealth, political power and public veneration.

T. E. Lawrence, in his book *The Seven Pillars of Wisdom* (Ch. 3, p.12, 13), describes the effect of living in the desert on people's views of life.

> They were a people of primary colours, or rather black and white, who saw the world always in contour. They were a dogmatic people, despising doubt... The common base was the ever-present idea of world-worthlessness ... Their profound reaction from matter led them to teach barrenness, renunciation, poverty.

Lawrence makes the point that they sought the desert not because they found God there but because 'in its solitude they heard more certainly the living word they brought with them'. It is as though the desert has a capacity to simplify consciousness itself.

The Tetrach of Galilee, Herod Antipas, arrested John the Baptist. By the standards set by the Herodian dynasty he was probably the most just. He had married the daughter of the Nabataen Arab king Arets IV to ensure peace between Jewish and Arab neighbours. After thirty years on the throne and approaching middle age he fell in love with his niece Herodias. She was the daughter of Herod the Great's son Aristobulos and was married to Philip, Antipas' half-brother. Herodias insisted that Antipas first divorced his wife but she was very reluctant to leave. Eventually she fled to her father. After their marriage, John the Baptist criticised Antipas, 'It is not lawful for you to have your brother's wife' (Matthew 14.4; Mark 6.18). According to the Torah, 'If a man takes his brother's wife it is impurity' (Lev. 20.21). Josephus gives another reason for John's imprisonment:

> Herod, who feared lest the great influence John had over the people might put it into his power and inclination to raise a rebellion (for they seemed ready to do anything he should advise), thought it best, by putting him to death, to prevent any mischief he might cause (Josephus, *Antiquities,* 18:5:2).

Antipas would have been concerned over John's teaching of an imminent new kingdom. Furthermore, Luke (3.12–14) states that tax collectors and soldiers were being baptized. They were Antipas' main source of revenue and security. Clearly John the Baptist was a potential threat.

After John's arrest, Jesus returned to Galilee. Whilst John was in prison his disciples recounted the miracles and teaching of Jesus. John clearly had serious doubts about Jesus in spite of God's apparent endorsement of him at his baptism. He sends two of his disciples to ask Jesus, 'Are you he who is to come, or shall we look for another?' (Matt. 11,3; Luke 7.19). Jesus did not conform to John's vision of the Messiah as one executing judgement with the destruction of the morally wayward. Furthermore, John's asceticism has been rejected. 'For John the Baptist has come eating no bread and drinking no wine. The Son of man has come eating and drinking'. Jesus is then described as 'a glutton and a drunkard, a friend of tax collectors and sinners' (Matt. 11.18–19; Luke 7.33–34).

Jesus' response is:

> Go and tell John what you have seen and heard: the blind receive their sight, the lame walk, lepers are cleansed, and the deaf hear, the dead are raised up, the poor have good news preached to them. And blessed is he who takes no offence at me (Matthew 11.5; Luke 7.22).

This is combination of two prophetic extracts from the Book of Isaiah (35.5–6; 61.1). Jesus does not answer the question directly but believes that these healings indicate the nearness or the presence of the Kingdom. The wonders of the final age as described in the Old Testament also appear in the Dead Sea Scrolls and may have been part of contemporary thought. In other words, Jesus is essentially saying, 'you should draw your own conclusions once you have heard what is happening around me. Do not be distressed if things are not turning out in accordance with your plan.'

Jesus paints a warm, loving picture of John the Baptist to the crowds concluding with the words:

> What then did you go to see? A prophet? Yes, I tell you, and more than a prophet. This is he of whom it is written, 'Behold, I send my messenger before thy face, who shall prepare thy way before thee.' I tell you among those born of women none is greater than John; yet he who is least in the kingdom of God is greater than he (Matthew 11.9–11).

The quotation is taken from Malachi (3.1) and is a variation of the text. The original says, 'He shall prepare *the* way before *me*'. Malachi thought that Isaiah was the messenger preparing the way for God himself to intervene directly, with no concept of a Messiah.

Antipas and his courtiers celebrated his birthday at a banquet with Herodias and her daughter, Salome, who was married to the Tetrach Philip. Salome 'came in and she danced and pleased Herod' to such an extent that he said, 'Ask of me for whatever you wish, and I will grant it, even half my kingdom'. After consulting her mother, Salome said, 'I want you to give me at once the head of John the Baptist on a platter'. Reluctantly, Herod Antipas conceded her request and a guard duly presented her with John the Baptist's head on a platter (Mark 6.21–28). The dance of the seven veils was a later elaboration and John the Baptist's head became one of the most prized Christian relics. At least five shrines claim to contain the original. Later, when Herod Antipas heard of Jesus' teaching and miracles he feared that John had been resurrected from the dead (Mark 6.14).

VI

Jesus the Charismatic Exorcist and Healer

Jesus' reputation as a healer is summarised by Matthew (4.23–25):

And he went about all Galilee, teaching in their synagogues and preaching the gospel of the kingdom and healing every disease and every infirmity among the people. So his fame spread throughout Syria, and they brought him all the sick, those afflicted with various diseases and pains, demoniacs, epileptics and paralytics, and he healed them. And great crowds followed him from Galilee and the Decapolis and Jerusalem and Judea and from beyond the Jordan.

Before discussing the New Testament accounts it is useful to put these in the historical context in which they were written. These include Greek culture, the Old Testament understanding of illness, and a Galilean devout sect within Judaism around the time of Jesus.

In the prevailing Greek culture of the time it was natural to believe that spiritual forces could affect the physical world in tangible ways. Miracles were perceived as a fact of life. Around the Mediterranean there were shrines to the Greek god Asclepius who was believed to have healing powers, and accounts of miraculous cures survive. Apollonius of Tyana was a noted exorcist and the accounts bear close similarity to those in the New Testament.

The Jews believed that God alone determined sickness or health. 'I kill and I make alive; I wound and I heal' (Deut. 32.39) or 'I am the Lord, your healer' (Exod. 15.26). King Asa's death is attributed to himself, 'even in his disease he did not seek the Lord, but sought help from the physicians' (2 Chron. 16.12).The attitude is made clear in Ecclesiasticus, (Ben Sira) 38.9–12 JB:

My son, when you are ill, do not be depressed,
    but pray to the Lord that he will heal you.
Renounce your faults, keep your hands unsoiled,
    and cleanse your heart from all sin.
Offer an incense and a memorial of fine flower,
    and make as rich an offering as you can afford.
Then let the doctor take over- the Lord created him too–
    and do not let him leave you, for you need him.

Pre-eminence is given to the Lord as healer. The section ends with, 'If a man sins in the eyes of his Maker, may he fall under the care of the doctor'. When faced with illness, the sequence is to pray, ask forgiveness, make a sacrifice then consult a doctor. Doctors at that time would have had very few useful skills or knowledge. Faced with illness, the only appropriate response was to turn to God and seek forgiveness. Sickness and sin become the two sides of the same coin. Conversely, healing and the forgiveness of sins were regarded as being closely related.

More pertinent were the Galilean Hasidim or the Devout, a charismatic sect within Judaism, who lived around the time of Jesus and are recorded in rabbinic literature. Geza Vermes describes the Hasidim in *Jesus the Jew*. They were analogous to the prophets of the Old Testament. Their direct relationship with God gave them supernatural powers. One example is Hanina ben Dosa, who resided in Arab, a city about ten miles north of Nazareth. He lived in the first century AD prior to the fall of Jerusalem in 70 AD. He was regarded as a man of extraordinary devotion and miraculous healing abilities. He is depicted as spending a full hour on directing his heart towards his Father in heaven before starting his prayer. Nothing would interrupt his concentration: 'Though the king salute him, he shall not return his greeting'. On one occasion, whilst he was praying, a poisonous snake bit him. He was unharmed but the snake died. Witnesses said, 'Woe to the man bitten by a snake, but woe to the snake which has bitten Rabbi Hanina ben Dosa'. When Hanina was told of the alarming incident he responded, 'May evil befall me if in the concentration of my heart I even felt it'. In an alternative version he says, 'It is not the snake that kills, but sin' (Vermes, 2001, p. 54–55). In other words, total trust in God and communion with him rendered the holy man immune. There is a parallel in the teaching of Jesus, 'Behold, I have given you authority to tread upon serpents and scorpions, and over all the power of the enemy; and nothing shall hurt you' (Luke 10.19).

Hanina was primarily famed for God's apparent willingness to respond to his prayers and heal the sick. Yohanan ben Zakkai, a community chief sought Hanina's help when his son fell ill: 'Hanina, my son, pray for him that he may live'. Hanina put his head between his knees and prayed; and the son lived. Yohanan's response was, 'Though ben Zakkai had squeezed his head between his knees all day long, no attention would have been paid to him' (Vermes 2001 p.55–56).

One story in particular illustrates Hanina's reputation. Gamaliel was the most highly regarded Pharisee in Jerusalem; Paul had been one of his pupils (Acts 22.3). His son became critically ill with a high fever. Gameliel sent two of his pupils to Hanina's home in Galilee. There, Hanina retired to an upper room and prayed, returning with the words, 'Go home for the fever has departed him'. The sceptical pupils asked whether he was a prophet. He replied modestly:

'I am no prophet, nor am I a prophet's son, but this is how I am favoured. If my prayer is fluent in my mouth, I know that he [the sick man] is favoured; if not, I know that it [the disease] is fatal' (Vermes, 2001, p.55–56).

It later transpired that the son of Gamaliel had been cured at the moment Hanina prayed. This story has similarities with Jesus healing the centurion's son (or, in some versions, servant) who was paralysed or 'sick at the point of death' (Matt. 8.5–13; Luke 7.1–10; John 4.46–54). The healing occurs at some distance from the ill person, and Hanina sensed the efficacy of his cure by the fluency of his speech. Jesus was aware when the 'woman who had a flow of blood for twelve years' touched his garments that 'power had gone out of him' (Mark 5.30; Luke 8.46).

Hanina ben Dosa is recorded as having control over evil spirits and natural phenomena such as rain. There are two other Hasidic traditions exemplified by Hanina. The first was a complete disregard for personal possessions amounting to a positive embrace of poverty and total reliance on God. They 'hated their own money, and all the more, the mammon of other people'. Their piety is summarised in the sentence: 'What is mine is yours and what is yours is your own' (Vermes, 2001, p.58). This belief is echoed in the New Testament, 'Foxes have holes, and birds of the air have nests; but the Son of man has nowhere to lay his head' (Matt. 8.20; Luke 9.58). The second tradition was an emphasis on moral behaviour rather than legal and ritual affairs. The phrase, 'The fear of the Lord is the beginning of wisdom' (Prov. 9.10; Ps. 111.10) is expounded in the Mishnah as:

> Any man whose fear of sin precedes his wisdom, his wisdom will endure; but if his wisdom precedes his fear of sin, his wisdom will not endure (Vermes, 1973, p.59).

In this context, wisdom is used to signify expertise in the Law. Fear of sin is more difficult. In the Temple there was a chamber of secrets filled with gifts or alms. Recipients could collect their due in secret but more importantly the donors would remain anonymous so that there was no possibility of them contributing so as to enhance their reputation. Such donors were described as sin fearing. Thus fear of sin is not some ascetic approach but the positive performance of good deeds in such a way that they cannot be seen by others as self-aggrandisement.

It is in this ethos of the Hasidim present in Galilee in the three centuries around the life of Jesus, that the miracle stories of the New Testament are best considered. They fall into three categories, exorcism, healing the sick and those related to the natural world.

Jesus the Exorcist

All three Synoptic Gospels make numerous references to Jesus casting out demons, although John's Gospel makes no reference to such deeds nor do they feature in the Old Testament.

Jesus exorcised a man with an "unclean spirit" in the synagogue in Capernaum. Mark writes (as does Luke 4.33–35):

> But Jesus rebuked him, saying, 'Be silent, and come out of him!' And the unclean spirit, convulsing him and crying with a loud voice, came out of him (Mark 1.23–26).

Some of the women who accompanied Jesus had been exorcised including Mary Magdalene 'from whom seven demons had gone out' (Luke 8.2).

In the country of the Gerasenes, Jesus met:

> ...a man with an unclean spirit, who lived among the tombs; and no one could bind him anymore, even with a chain; for he had often been bound with fetters and chains, but the chains he wrenched apart, and the fetters he broke in pieces; and no one had the strength to subdue him. Night and day among the tombs and on the mountains he was always crying out, and bruising himself with stones (Mark 5.1–13; Matt 8.28–31; Luke 8.26–32).

Jesus first says, 'Come out of the man, you unclean spirit', but as there appears no response he asks, 'What is your name?'

He replied, 'My name is Legion; for we are many,' Knowing the name was part of the ritual of exorcism. The spirits beg Jesus not to send them out of the country but rather that they be sent into a herd of swine. The herd 'numbering about two thousand, rushed down the steep bank into the sea, and were drowned'. Exorcism was often associated with some physical sign that the demons had left. The herdsmen returned to the town and people came to see what had happened. The demoniac was seen 'clothed and in his right mind'. The people implored Jesus to leave the neighbourhood, hardly a surprising reaction after the loss of so many swine. One must question why there was a herd of two thousand pigs in Galilee. Jewish law was clear, 'Of their flesh [swine] you shall not eat, and their carcasses you shall not touch; they are unclean to you' (Lev. 11.8). This rule was strictly obeyed. When the servants of Antiochus Epiphanes tried to force Eleazar to eat pig's flesh he chose death rather than break the Law (2 Macc. 6.18–31 JB). The pigs must have belonged to Gentiles living in the area. The location of the incident is difficult to explain. Mark and Luke refer to the country of the Gerasenes, but Gerasa is about thirty miles south east of the Sea of Galilee with no significant mass of water in the area. Matthew refers to the Gadarenes but Gadara is six miles from the sea.

In the region of Tyre and Sidon, Jesus reluctantly exorcises a demon from the daughter of a Syrophoenician (Matthew describes her as a Canaanite) woman. The daughter was not physically present being at home at the time (Mark 7.24–30; Matthew 15.21–28).

And he [Jesus] said to her, 'Let the children first be fed, for it is not right to take the children's bread and throw it to the dogs'. But she answered him, 'Yes, Lord; yet even the dogs under the table eat the children's crumbs.'

Matthew here sees Jesus' mission to be directed to the Jews and not to the Gentiles who were symbolised as dogs. Matthew is quite explicit when he quotes Jesus: 'I was sent only to the lost sheep of the house of Israel'. Jesus makes an exception here, 'For this saying you may go your way; the demon has left your daughter'. Jesus' attitude towards Gentiles will be considered later.

There is an account of an epileptic boy whom the disciples had failed to exorcise (Matthew 17.14–18; Mark 9.15–27; Luke 9.38–42). They took the boy to Jesus and the spirit 'convulsed the boy, and he fell on the ground and rolled about foaming at the mouth'.

91

And Jesus asked his father, 'How long has he had this?' And he said, 'From childhood. And it has often cast him into the fire and into the water, to destroy him; but if you can do anything, have pity on us and help us.' And Jesus said to him, 'If you can! All things are possible to him who believes.' Immediately the father of the child cried out and said, 'I believe; help my unbelief!' And when Jesus saw that a crowd came running together, he rebuked the unclean spirit, saying to it, 'You dumb and deaf spirit, I command you, come out of him, and never enter him again.' And after crying out and convulsing him terribly, it came out, and the boy was like a corpse; so that most of them said, 'He is dead.' but Jesus took him by the hand and lifted him up, and he arose (Mark 9.21–27).

Mark's account is so vivid and true to life. Only in Mark does Jesus ask, 'How long has he had this?' Matthew and Luke would not contemplate any lack of knowledge by Jesus.

The disciples on the way to Capernaum had been discussing who amongst them was the greatest. Mark (9.33–34) has Jesus asking, 'What were you discussing on the way?' Matthew (18.1) doesn't pose the question. Luke (9.47) states, 'Jesus perceived the thought of their hearts'. There is something so natural about the distraught father's request, 'If you can do anything' and Jesus' response, 'If you can!' This is the only occasion Jesus is recorded as saying to the spirit, 'never enter him again!' However it was believed that an exorcised demon could return to the same person and Jesus uses the analogy in the parable of the return of the unclean spirit (Matthew 12.44–45; Luke 11.24–26). Josephus describes the exorcist Eleazar forbidding the demon to return. The implication was that exorcism might result in a remission rather than a cure.

There are two other accounts, omitted by Mark, of exorcism. Luke writes:

Now he was casting out a demon that was dumb; but when the demon had gone out, the dumb man spoke, and the people marvelled. But some of them said, 'He casts out demons by Beelzebul, the prince of demons,' while others to test him, sought from him a sign from heaven (Luke 11.14–16).

Matthew (9.32–34) gives a similar account and later (12.22–24) of a blind and dumb demoniac. Beelzebul literally means Prince Baal (2 Kings 1.2) but is derisively spelt Beelzebub or Lord of the Flies in some early manuscripts. Jesus refutes the suggestion that he is using the power of Beelzebul as Satan would not be so foolish as to raise civil war in his own realm.

Jesus uses the vocabulary of other exorcists of the time such as 'come out', 'be silent' and 'Ephphata' or 'be opened'. His twelve disciples undertook exorcisms, 'And he appointed twelve, to be with him, and to be sent out to preach and to have authority to cast out demons' (Mark 3.14–15). 'And they [the disciples] cast out many demons, and anointed with oil many that were sick and healed them' (Mark 6.13).

Later Jesus appointed seventy others and sent them ahead of him in pairs:

The seventy returned with joy, saying, 'Lord, even the demons are subject to us in your name!' (Luke 10.17).

There were other exorcists in Galilee. John says:

'Master, we saw a man casting out demons in your name, and we forbade him, because he does not follow with us.' Jesus responds, 'Do not forbid him; for he that is not against you is for you' (Luke 9.49–50).

St Paul continued the practice. When Paul was in Ephesus, 'some of the itinerant Jewish exorcists undertook to pronounce the name of the Lord Jesus over those who had evil spirits' (Acts 19.13).

In the ancient world, the belief in demons and demonic possession was part of the culture. In the time of Origen (c. 185–254 AD) the exorcist ranked third in the grade of orders of the clergy. John Wesley was founder of the Methodist Church. His journals often ascribed phenomena that accompanied his preaching to demon possession (Wesley's Journal for Oct 25th 1739). According to a Papal decree, to this day each of the three thousand Catholic Church Dioceses worldwide must have among the ranks of its priests a trained exorcist.

Although exorcism is still practiced by a few it is no longer considered a valid explanation of the phenomena seen. This is not to deny that some dramatic cures or remissions were witnessed at the time. Rather, our interpretation of such events would be to ascribe them to conditions such as epilepsy, hysteria or schizophrenia rather than to demon possession. In ancient times such phenomena were believed to be the powers of good and evil spirits and to them such occurrences were credible.

Jesus the Healer

The Synoptic Gospels emphasise the healing abilities of Jesus. Matthew writes:

And great crowds came to him, bringing with them the lame, the maimed, the blind, the dumb, and many others, and they put them at his feet, and he healed them, so that the throng wondered, when they saw the dumb speaking, the maimed whole, the lame walking, the blind seeing; and they glorified the God of Israel (Matthew 15.30–31).

He also reinforces his message by using a *pesher*, quoting Isaiah 53.4: 'This was to fulfil what was spoken by the prophet Isaiah, "He took our infirmities and bore our diseases"' (Matthew 8.17).

The Synoptic Gospels give about fifteen specific incidents of healing. There are some differences between the gospel accounts and we cannot be always sure whether they refer to the same incident or separate occasions. The illnesses were diverse, encompassing the blind man in Bethsaida, Bartimaeus, eleven men with leprosy, fever, haemorrhage (menorrhagia), a withered arm, a deaf mute, a centurion's paralysed servant (or son in some versions), a paralysed man lowered down from the roof, a woman who had been bent over for eighteen years and a man with dropsy.

There are a number of themes that recur through these healing narratives. The concept that sin and sickness were manifestations of evil and the interrelatedness of the two has already been discussed. The most consistent feature is the faith of the individual approaching Jesus. Bartimaeus, the blind beggar receives his sight and Jesus tells him, 'Go your way your faith has made you well' (Mark 10.52). Two blind men approach him and:

> Jesus said to them 'Do you believe that I am able to do this?' They said to him 'Yes, Lord.'. Then he touched their eyes, saying, 'According to your faith be it done to you' (Matthew 9.27–31).

After curing ten lepers, only one, a Samaritan, returned to give thanks. Jesus says, 'Rise and go your way; your faith has made you well' (Luke 17.19). The woman with twelve years' history of menorrhagia touched Jesus' garment with immediate relief of symptoms. Jesus says, 'Daughter, your faith has made you well, go in peace and be healed of your disease' (Mark 5.34). A paralysed man is lowered from a roof to gain access to Jesus. 'And when Jesus saw their faith, he said to the paralytic, 'My son your sins are forgiven' (Matthew 9.1–8; Mark 2.1–12; Luke 5.17–26). A centurion asks Jesus to heal his paralysed servant, which he does in absentia with the words, 'Go, be it done for you as you have believed' (Matt. 8.13). Luke, for his Gentile audience, inserts that the centurion had built a synagogue (Luke 7.5).

The faith is not a set of doctrines but simply a trust in him and confidence that he can help. Jesus is self-effacing, attributing the miraculous cures to the faith of the patient rather than his own powers. There are occasions when he commands those cured not to tell anyone. Thus the two blind men are told, 'See that no one knows it'. However, 'They spread his fame throughout the district' (Matthew 9.30–31. A similar command

95

and response occurred after healing the deaf mute (Mark 7.36). This emphasis on faith is reiterated in Mark (6.4–6):

> And Jesus said to them, 'A prophet is not without honour, except in his own country, and among his own kin, and in his own house.' And he could do no mighty works there, except that he laid his hands upon a few sick people and healed them. And they marvelled because of their unbelief.

Unlike exorcism, healing usually involved physical contact with the person. The two blind men near Jericho begged to have their sight restored 'And Jesus in pity touched their eyes, and immediately they received their sight and followed him' (Matt. 20.34). Jesus in treating the blind man at Bethsaida 'spat on his eyes and laid his hands on him' (Mark 8.23).The man with leprosy was healed when 'he stretched out his hand and touched him' (Luke 5.13). Simon's mother-in-law lay sick with fever 'And he came and took her by the hand and lifted her up and the fever left her' (Mark 1.31). For the deaf mute 'he put his fingers into his ears, and he spat and touched his tongue' (Mark 7.33). He laid his hands on the woman who was bent over (Luke 13:13). The woman with haemorrhage touched his garment but Jesus was aware 'that power had gone forth from him' (Mark 5.30).

There are two resurrection accounts. Jairus, a president of a synagogue, approaches Jesus saying, 'My little daughter is at the point of death'. Others arrive to announce that she had died. Jesus went to the house and said, 'Why do you make a tumult and weep? The child is not dead, but sleeping'. Then, 'taking her by the hand he said to her, "Talitha cum", which means, "Little girl, I say to you, arise". And immediately the girl sat up and walked' (Matt. 9.18–19, 23–26; Mark 5.22–24, 35–43; Luke 8.41–42, 49–56). Luke omits the Aramaic, 'Talitha cum'. He may have thought that his Greek-speaking non-Jewish readers could have interpreted this as a magical incantation. He also includes the phrase that 'her spirit returned', indicating a resurrection from the dead rather than an awakening from deep sleep. We are left in doubt about the authors' view as to whether or not this was a true resurrection. Both Mark and Luke include the command, 'And he strictly charged them that no one should know this'. Matthew on the other hand says, 'And the report of this went through all the district'. Both could be true if Jesus' command was disregarded.

Only Luke (7.11–17) recalls the story of Jesus encountering the funeral procession of the only son of a widow in Nain. It was the custom at the time to bury the dead before the next sunset and so he would have died recently. Jesus touched the bier and said, 'Young man I say to you arise'. The dead man sat up and began to speak. Luke continues:

> Fear seized them all; and they glorified God, saying, 'A great prophet has arisen among us!' and 'God has visited his people!' And this report concerning him spread through the whole of Judaea and all the surrounding country'.

What resonates so strongly is Luke's concept of Jesus being the new Elijah. The account corresponds so closely to Elijah restoring a dead son to a widowed mother (1 Kings 17.17–24) and a similar miracle attributed to Elisha (2 Kings 4.18–37). This may well be another example of the use of a *pesher* to expound on the life of Jesus.

John's gospel (11.1–53) narrates the raising of Lazarus, four days after his death. There is no mention of this in the Synoptic Gospels. This is surprising as Lazarus was not an obscure individual but the brother of Mary and Martha. Luke recalls that when Jesus stayed with them, Mary got very angry when she was busy preparing a meal alone whilst Martha sat talking to Jesus. When Lazarus was taken ill and the two sisters sent for Jesus, he delayed his departure. Jesus tells his disciples that, 'Lazarus is dead; and for your sake I am glad that I was not there, so that you might believe'. The implication being that he could then perform a greater miracle. John's account is full of theological imagery and a prelude to Jesus' crucifixion. Lazarus had been in the tomb for four days. Traditional belief at the time was that the spirit remained near the body for three days and then departed. Travelling to Bethany, the home of Lazarus, was fraught with danger as, 'the Jews were but now seeking to stone you'. Such was the implied threat that Thomas says, 'Let us also go that we may die with him'. Later Jesus reassures Martha, 'I am the resurrection and the life; he who believes in me, though he die, yet shall he live, and whoever lives and believes in me shall never die'. Martha responds, 'Yes, Lord; I believe that you are the Christ, the Son of God, he who is coming into the world'.

The concept of 'Son of God' will be discussed later. That this confession of faith would have been uttered during his lifetime is implausible but it provides a clear opportunity for John to succinctly summarise his theological understanding of Jesus and his subsequent crucifixion. It would be entirely rational to regard this miracle as a theological parable expressed as a historical event.

In all the healing miracles the association between sin, illness and the need for repentance is clear with one exception. John (9.1–41) describes Jesus restoring of sight of a man blind from birth. The disciples ask him, 'Rabbi, who sinned, this man or his parents, that he was born blind?' Jesus answered, 'It was not that this man sinned, or his parents, but that the works of God might be made manifest in him.' In other words, he was blind so that a miracle may be performed. Perhaps this exception confirms the rule.

The close relationship between disease or deformity and sin is exemplified in the rules applying to priests as described in Leviticus 21. 18–21:

For no one who has a blemish shall draw near [the veil or the altar of the temple], a man blind or lame, or one who has a mutilated face or a limb too long, or a man who has an injured foot or an injured hand, or a hunchback, or a dwarf, or a man with a defect in his sight or an itching disease or scabs or crushed testicles'. Such people would profane my [God's] sanctuaries.

Such disabilities were a sign of underlying sin.

The belief became deeply embedded in our psychology. Down the ages the cripple has been regarded as a curse of God and consequently has been killed, persecuted, ridiculed or neglected. Well known examples include Quasimodo in Hugo's, *The Hunchback of Notre Dame*, the black dwarf in the novel of the same name by Walter Scott, and John Merrick, "the elephant man". Within living memory, in Upper Parliament Street Liverpool, there was a large derelict Victorian red brick building. A large sign remained above the entrance, The Liverpool Institution for the Incurables. Here children with physical deformities would be incarcerated and not considered even worthy of any education. Their deformities represented punishment for some terrible sin committed by perhaps an ancestor. The Victorians saw no reason why their suffering should be mitigated. Fortunately a more enlightened view has prevailed but the origin of such beliefs has a Biblical basis.

It is misleading to compare Jesus with pagan magicians such as Apollonius of Tyana and occult practices described in the Greek Magical Papyri. Rather, one can regard his actions in the context of contemporary Galilean charismatic Judaism. Jesus could be regarded as the paramount example of the early Hasidim or Devout. These were men who appeared to have supernatural abilities derived not from magical powers but from immediate contact with God. The people regarded these holy men as part of the long prophetic tradition.

The Nature Miracles

The nature miracles are few in number but resonate with events in the Old Testament. There was a popular belief at the time that Jesus was a prophet. Jesus asked his disciples, 'Who do men say that I am?' And they told him, 'John the Baptist; and others say Elijah; and others one of the prophets' (Mark 8.27–28). To be convinced that Jesus was a prophet they required some divine sign comparable to their deliverance from Egypt by Moses. Alternatively, Elijah when confronting the prophets of Baal on Mount Carmel sacrificed a bull, placed it with firewood on a stone altar and then soaked everything with water. In response to his prayers, 'the fire of the Lord fell, and consumed the burnt offering, and the wood and the stones, and the dust, and licked up the water that was in the trench' (1 Kings 18.38). Isaiah produced a sign from the Lord when the shadow from a sundial went backwards (2 Kings 20.8–11). Jesus' response to such requests was to 'sigh deeply in his spirit' and to say, 'Why does this generation seek a sign? Truly, I say to you, no sign shall be given to this generation' (Mark 8.12). In spite of this, the authors do describe some nature miracles.

According to John (2.1–11) Jesus' first miracle or to use John's words, 'the first of his signs', was at a marriage at Cana in Galilee when the wine ran out. Jesus instructed that six stone jars be filled with water. The jars were usually used for Jewish rites of purification such as washing guests' feet or hands prior to eating. Each held twenty or thirty gallons. When the steward tasted the content of the jars he found that the water had been changed into wine. This became a highly symbolic act. The water for ritual purification representing Mosaic Law became the wine giving joy to the wedding celebration representing the kingdom of God. One can only speculate as to what extent John wished us to understand the account as historical or allegorical.

After Jesus had calmed a storm on the Sea of Galilee his disciples said, 'Who then is this, that even the wind and the sea obey him?' (Matthew 8.24–27; Mark 4.37–41; Luke 8.24–25). Jesus' power over the elements reflects the imagery particularly of the Psalms: 'Thou dost rule the raging of the sea; when its waves rise, thou stillest them' (Ps. 89.9; 65.7; 107.23–30). On another occasion the disciples were having difficulty rowing their boat against a strong wind. Jesus walked to them on the sea and they thought it was a ghost: 'And he got into the boat and the wind ceased' (Matthew 14.22–27; 31–33; Mark 6.45–52). There was an unexpectedly large catch of fish by Simon (Peter) and his colleagues after Jesus had instructed them to, 'Put out into the deep and let down your nets for a catch' (Luke 5.2–11). Jesus then says to Simon, 'Do not be afraid, henceforth you will be catching men'. The analogy between men and fish figures in the Old Testament.

For thou makest men like the fish of the sea, like crawling things that have no ruler. He brings them up with a hook, he drags them out with his net (Habakkuk 1.14–15).

'Behold, I am sending for many fishers, says the Lord, and they shall catch them' (Jer. 16.16). However the fishermen of the Old Testament were hostile figures sent to punish the wicked whereas Jesus uses the idiom to refer to saviours.

Matthew includes a polemic about paying taxes (17.24–27). Every Jew was expected to pay half a shekel towards the maintenance of the Temple, which Jesus did. The argument is a little confused as Matthew was writing after the destruction of the Temple and the Romans, under Domitian, continued to collect the Temple tax for their own purpose which to the Jews would have been iniquitous. However Jesus resolves the issue by saying, 'However, not to give offence to them, go to the sea and cast a hook, and take the first fish that comes up, and when you open its mouth you will find a shekel; take that and give it to them for me and for yourself'. Jesus would not have faced this dilemma in his lifetime.

Mark (6.33–44; 8.1–9) records two occasions when Jesus fed a large crowd with only a few loaves and some fish. Both Matthew (14.13–21; 15.32–38) and Luke (9.10–17) record the story with minor variations. All accounts recall that after the crowds were satisfied they collected 'baskets full of broken pieces and of the fish'. None of the accounts record any reaction of amazement by the crowds, which is surprising when compared to other miracle stories. The crowds were large but perhaps the figure of five thousand men besides women and children appears a little exaggerated. On the other hand, perhaps there is a deeper symbolism. The five thousand represented the Jewish nation and the twelve Jewish narrow-necked baskets (*kophinos*) representing the twelve tribes. The second incident took place in the Decapolis with a large gentile population and where four thousand were present and the remaining food collected in Greek hampers (*sphuris*) representing the Gentiles. We do not know what actually happened but what is certain is that the story echoes the Old Testament tradition. When Moses was leading the Israelites through the desert and they were starving he turned to God and 'In the evening quails came up and covered the camp'. In the morning the ground was covered with 'a fine, flake like thing' known as manna, the food of angels. Psalm 78 (23–25) refers to manna, 'And they ate and were well filled, for he [God] gave them what they craved'. Elisha with only twenty loaves of barley and fresh ears of grain asks his servant to share this among a hundred hungry men. The servant couldn't see how this could be done as barley loaves were like small hard buns. Nevertheless, he obliged 'And they ate, and had some left' (2 Kings 4.42–44).

No matter how we interpret or maybe dismiss the miracle stories the reality is that Jesus' contemporaries believed that he had extraordinary powers. It may be that with the passage of time the individual incidents were embellished to reflect the fulfilment of scriptural prophecy or given Christological significance. However, what is beyond doubt is that the people of the time, including his critics, never doubted his role as a miracle worker. Critics questioned his authority or motivation but not the miracles themselves. Even Josephus describes him thus:

Now, there was about this time, Jesus, a wise man, if it be lawful to call him a man, for he was a doer of wonderful works, a teacher of such men as receive the truth with pleasure (Josephus, *Antiquities,* 18:3.3).

Of equal importance, Jesus' close followers continued to perform miracles after his death, indicating that his power was still acting through them. Peter and John were going to the Temple to pray when a man lame from birth was being carried to the gate called Beautiful to ask for alms.

Peter said, 'I have no silver or gold, but I give you what I have; in the name of Jesus Christ of Nazareth, walk.' He immediately regained strength in his legs and walked into the Temple to praise God. The crowd were amazed but Peter addressed them, 'Men of Israel, why do you wonder at this, or why do you stare at us, as though by our own power or piety we had made him walk? ... And his name [Jesus], by faith in his name, has made this man strong whom you see and know; and the faith which is through Jesus has given the man this perfect health in the presence of you all' (Acts 3.1–16).

Jesus' miracles were not intended as an end in themselves, rather they were to convey a more profound message to the people. As previously mentioned, when John the Baptist was imprisoned he sent a messenger to ask Jesus whether he is 'the one to come' the reply was:

'Go and tell John what you hear and see; the blind receive their sight and the lame walk, lepers are cleansed and the deaf hear, and the dead are raised up, and the poor have good news preached to them' (Matthew 11.4–5; Luke 7.18–22).

Jesus is deliberately reminding his audience of Isaiah's prophecy that one day God would intervene and Israel would be redeemed and Jerusalem renewed. God's kingdom would be established on earth.

Say to those of a fearful heart, 'be strong, fear not! Behold, your God will come with vengeance, with the recompense of God. He will come to save you. Then the eyes of the blind shall be opened, and the ear of the deaf unstopped; then the lame man leap like a hart, and the tongue of the dumb sing for joy' (Isaiah 35.4–6).

'Thy dead shall live, their bodies shall rise' (Isaiah 26.19). The miracles were clear evidence that God's reign on earth had begun. 'If by the finger of God I cast out demons, then surely the Kingdom of God has come upon you' (Matt. 12.28; Luke 11.20). Without the evidence of the miracles it is unlikely that anyone would have taken Jesus' message to repent as the kingdom of God is at hand seriously.

VII

The Teaching of Jesus

The dominant theme in the Synoptic Gospels is Jesus' message that the kingdom of God was imminent. In the time of Jesus there was an expectation amongst Jews that God would intervene decisively in their predicament as he had done in their release from Egypt and on other occasions in the past. They believed in the vision of Isaiah, reiterated in the Psalms, that God would create his kingdom through the Jews and only then would Gentiles turn to the kingdom.

> The wealth of Egypt and the merchandise of Ethiopia, and the Sabeans, men of stature, shall come over to you; they shall come over in chains and bow down to you. They will make supplication to you, saying: 'God is with you only, and there is no other, no god besides him' (Isaiah 45.14).

The recognition of the God of Israel by the Gentiles would also imply their submission to the Jews, 'With their faces to the ground they shall bow down to you, and lick the dust of your feet' (Isaiah 49.23). Isaiah's vision is expounded further in chapter 60:

> But the Lord will arise on you, and his glory will be seen upon you. And nations shall come to your light, and kings to the brightness of your rising... The wealth of nations shall come to you... They shall bring gold and frankincense, and shall proclaim the praise of the

Lord... They shall come up with acceptance on my altar, and I will glorify my glorious house (Isaiah 60.2–7).

The author of Daniel (c.164 BC) wrote:

The God of heaven will set up a kingdom which will never be destroyed, nor shall its sovereignty be left to any other people. It will break in pieces all those kingdoms and bring them to an end, and it will stand for ever (Daniel 2.44).

Jesus not only shared this belief but it was the key message that infused all his teaching. We will return to Jesus' understanding of the kingdom of God in more detail later. To place it in context we need to explore Jesus' understanding of Judaism.

Jesus and Mosaic Law

Jesus is quite clear in his affirmative attitude to the Mosaic Law: 'But it is easier for heaven and earth to pass away, than for one dot of the law to become void' (Luke 16.17) Furthermore he says:

For truly, I say to you, till heaven and earth pass away, not an iota, not a dot, will pass from the law until all is accomplished. Whoever then relaxes one of the least of the commandments and teaches men so, shall be called least in the kingdom of heaven; but he who does them and teaches them shall be called great in the kingdom of heaven (Matthew 5.18–19).

Such categorical statements would have been an embarrassment to the early Gentile Christians. The authors would not have included such statements were there not a strong tradition that this was what Jesus taught. Both authors appear to add caveats to make the statements more acceptable to a Gentile audience, for example:

The law and the prophets were until John; since then the good news of the kingdom of God is preached, and everyone enters it violently. But it is easier for heaven and earth to pass away, than for one dot of the law to become void (Luke 16.16–17).

Matthew acknowledges the Mosaic Law as appertaining 'until all is accomplished'. Theologians may argue about the precise meaning of these verses, but their essential validity is revealed in Jesus' own actions and teaching.

Jesus attends the synagogue and teaches there:

And they went into Capernaum; and immediately on the Sabbath he entered the synagogue and taught. And they were astonished at his teaching, for he taught them as one who had authority, and not as the scribes (Mark 1.21–22; Luke 4.31).

In Galilee, 'he taught in their synagogues, being glorified by all' (Luke 4.15). There is special reference to his reading from Isaiah in the synagogue in Nazareth (Luke 4.16–20). In addition Jesus makes the pilgrimage to Jerusalem to celebrate the festival of the Passover. According to John, he attends on five occasions, thrice for Passover (2.13; 6.4; 11.55), once for an unspecified feast (5.1), once for Sukkot (7.2,10) when he stays until the Feast of Dedication (10.22). On these occasions he would have been in Jerusalem for the weeklong rite of purification, bathing on the third and seventh day in the special pools and being sprinkled with the ashes of a sacrificed red heifer. There he is no idle bystander but 'he was teaching daily in the Temple' (Luke 19.47). Jesus makes arrangements to share the Passover meal with his disciples in accordance with Mosaic Law. They would all have had to be purified to partake in the meal and one of them would have been to the Temple that day to sacrifice the lamb or goat.

A further example of Jesus endorsing Mosaic Law was his instruction to the leper whom he healed, 'show yourself to the priest, and offer for your cleansing what Moses commanded' (Mark 1.40–44). There were specific rules for cleansing lepers as detailed in Leviticus 14.1–32. First the leper is examined by the priest and if he appears to have been healed a bird is killed in an earthen vessel over running water. A live bird is then dipped in the blood of the dead bird and released. The running water and the release of the bird were symbols of the removal of uncleanness. The remaining blood is sprinkled seven times over the leper. The leper then washes his clothes, shaves off all bodily hair and bathes. He then lives for seven days outside his tent before returning to the priest having shaven and bathed again. On the eighth day the leper offers two male lambs, one ewe lamb, a cereal offering and oil. The priest uses these to follow the detailed protocol of slaughter, anointing, sprinkling and burning. If the leper is too poor he can offer one male lamb, cereal, oil and two turtle doves or two young pigeons. This may seem strange to us today but the Jews in the time of Jesus would have known precisely what he meant when he said 'show yourself to the priest'. Jesus would have had no impact had he not spoken in terms that his audience were familiar with.

There are however instances when Jesus is criticised for his interpretation of Mosaic Law. The Pharisees criticised Jesus' disciples for not washing their hands before meals (Mark 7.1–15; Matt. 15.1–11). Mosaic Law requires bathing before entering the Temple. The Pharisees added a purity rule insisting on the washing of hands before Sabbath and festival meals. This rule was later extended to all meals. This is not part of the Torah but represents the oral tradition introduced by the Pharisees. Thus the criticism regarding hand washing can be dismissed as trivial. However in the subsequent dialogue Jesus is quoted as saying, 'Do you not see that whatever goes into a man from outside cannot defile him, since it enters not his heart but his stomach, and so passes on?' (Thus he declared all foods clean.) And he said, 'What comes out of a man is what defiles a man. For within, out of the heart of man, come evil thoughts, fornication, theft, murder, adultery, coveting, wickedness, deceit, licentiousness, envy, slander, pride, foolishness' (Mark 7.18–22; Matthew 15.17–20). Matthew adds, 'To eat with unwashed hands does not defile a man'. What we have here is Jesus stressing the importance of moral attitudes summed up as pure of heart. That he declared all foods clean was not something adopted by the Palestinian Jesus movement which observed Mosaic Law. Peter similarly maintains that, 'I have never eaten anything that is common or unclean' (Acts 10.14). Jesus' statement that all foods were clean must be an addition to Mark's original text by a late redactor hence the parenthesis in the RSV Bible.

Similarly the disciples but not Jesus are accused of breaking the Sabbath by plucking heads of grain as they walked through the fields (Mark 2.23–28; Matthew 12.1–4; Luke 6.1–5). Jesus' defence is that the relief of hunger and the preservation of life took precedence over Sabbath law. David's soldiers ate the consecrated bread reserved for the priests when they were hungry (1 Sam. 21.1–7). Matthew adds the argument that priests continue to undertake sacrificial worship on the Sabbath with all the physical work this involves. The conclusion was that 'the Sabbath was made for man, not man for the Sabbath'. One has to question whether it had ever crossed the minds of these Galilean disciples that casually plucking heads of grain broke the Sabbath rule.

There are three occasions when Jesus healed on the Sabbath. All three Synoptic Gospels record a man with a withered hand (Mark 3.1–6; Matthew 12.9–14; Luke 6.6–11). Jesus simple asks him to stretch out his hand and it is restored. To his critics Jesus says, 'Is it lawful on a Sabbath to do good or to do harm, to save life or to kill?' Matthew adds, 'What man of you, if he has one sheep and it falls into a pit on a Sabbath, will not lay hold of it and lift it out? Of how much more value is a man than a sheep!' Luke (13.10–17) records a woman who had been bent over for eighteen years. Jesus laid his hands on her and she was able to straighten up. The ruler of the synagogue said that she should have sought healing during the week rather than on the Sabbath. Jesus responds, 'You hypocrites! Does not each of you on the Sabbath untie his ox or his ass from the manger, and lead it away to water it? And ought not this woman, a daughter of Abraham whom Satan bound for eighteen years, be loosed from this bond on the Sabbath day?' Jesus, whilst dining on the Sabbath at the house of a ruler who was a Pharisee, was presented with a man with dropsy. Jesus 'took him and healed him, and let him go' (Luke 14.1–6). In contrast John's gospel (5.1–18) describes Jesus curing a man who had been sick for thirty-eight years by the Pool of Bethzatha. Jesus said, 'Get up, pick up your sleeping-mat and walk.' What angered the authorities was not the healing but the command to carry his sleeping-mat on the Sabbath. These petty criticisms of Jesus cannot be used to suggest that he rejected the Torah.

There is a group of sayings that some Christian commentators interpret as rejecting the Law of Moses and the creation of a new ethic. They consist of six antitheses, but as the argument is the same in each case we need only consider the first.

> You have heard that it was said to the men of old, 'You shall not kill; and whoever kills shall be liable to judgement'. But I say to you that every one who is angry with his brother shall be liable to judgment; whoever insults his brother shall be liable to the council, and who ever says 'You fool!' shall be liable to the hell of fire' (Matthew 5.21–22).

What Jesus is emphasising is the need for a change in moral attitude thereby removing the cause of murder. If one is not angry with one's brother, one is not going to murder him. This is not a denial of one of the Ten Commandments but a deeper reinterpretation of it.

In summary, there is nothing in the gospel accounts of Jesus to suggest that he ever disregarded Mosaic Law. Furthermore, in all his teaching he endorses the validity of the Hebrew Scriptures. It is true that he interprets the texts in more profound ways, but anyone with the slightest knowledge of Judaism realises that one of its cardinal features is an enduring search for new interpretations as exemplified by numerous works in the Rabbinic period. *Aggadah* explains parables, maxims and anecdotes in traditional Jewish literature to illustrate the meaning or purpose of the law or custom. *Halakha* translated as 'the Law' or 'the path' that is based on what is not stated but has been derived from the TaNaKh. *Mishnah* preserved the oral traditions of the Pharisees from the Second Temple period (536 BC – 70 AD) and was redacted c. 220 AD. *Gemara*, was a rabbinical analysis and commentary on the *Mishnah.* A Palestinian version was completed about 350–400 AD and a Babylonian version in about 500 AD. The *Talmud* comprises the *Mishnah* as the core text and the *Gemara* as a commentary. This is the central text of Rabbinic Judaism.

The Kingdom of God

Mark summarises Jesus' message thus: 'The time is fulfilled, and the kingdom of God is at hand; repent and believe in the gospel' (Mark 1.15). The message is simple. In the near future God will rule the earth with the consequent radical reorientation of values and power. The Lord's Prayer includes, 'Your will be done on earth as it is in Heaven' (Matthew 6.10). At the beginning of this chapter the prophets' expectations were outlined. Yet Hebrew scripture is not clear as to whether God would intervene directly or use an intermediary. Nor is it clear whether or not the Jews will become a shining example to the rest of the world who in turn will acknowledge their God. Alternatively, their foes may be crushed by force. Such details are pure speculation as the expectation is that God will intervene and he will decide the method. The Synoptic Gospels portray Jesus' key message as man's urgent need to prepare for this event.

Jesus describes the essential conditions for entry into the kingdom. The first was repentance. This did not signify regret for past actions, rather it involved a complete reversal from all non-God centred activities. The Old Testament uses the words, 'turning away from' and John's gospel describes it as 'rebirth.' This was a profound personal commitment and transformation.

The second requirement was unconditional trust in God and his Providential care. To take one example:

And he [Jesus] said to his disciples, 'Therefore I tell you, do not be anxious about your life, what you shall eat, nor about your body, what you shall put on. For life is more than food and the body more than clothing. Consider the ravens: they neither sow nor reap, they have neither storehouse nor barn, and yet God feeds them. Of how much more value are you than the birds! And which of you by being anxious can add a cubit to his span of life? If then you are not able to do as small a thing as that, why are you anxious about the rest? Consider the lilies, how they grow; they neither toil nor spin; yet I tell you, even Solomon in all his glory was not arrayed like one of these. But if God so clothes the grass which is alive in the field today and tomorrow is thrown into the oven, how much more will he clothe you. O men of little faith? And do not seek what you are to eat and what you are to drink, nor be of anxious mind. For all the nations of the world seek these things; and your Father knows that you need them. Instead seek his kingdom, and these shall be yours as well' (Luke 12.22–31; Matthew 6.25–33).

This unconditional trust in God permeates the New Testament. Jesus exudes confidence in his followers:

Ask, and it will be given you; seek, and you will find; knock, and it will be opened to you. For everyone who asks receives, and he who seeks finds, and to him who knocks it will be opened (Luke 11.9–10; Matthew 7.7–8).

Similarly, 'Truly, I say to you, whoever says to this mountain, "Be taken up and cast into the sea," and does not doubt in his heart, but believes that what he says will come to pass, it will be done for him. Therefore I tell you, whatever you ask in prayer, believe that you receive it, and you will' (Mark 11.23–24; Matthew 17.20; 21:21; Luke 17.6).

Jesus uses the analogy of a child's trust in his father:

'Or what man of you, if his son asks him for a loaf, will give him a stone? Or if he asks for a fish, will give him a serpent? If you then, who are evil, know how to give good gifts to

111

your children, how much more will your Father who is in heaven give good things to those who ask him?' (Matthew 7.9,10; Luke 11.11–13).

The message is clear; unless one surrenders oneself completely to God's Providence one cannot enter the kingdom of God: 'Truly, I say to you, unless you turn and become like children, you will never enter the kingdom of heaven' (Matt. 18.3).

Certain corollaries follow. Jesus demands unreserved devotion to the task of preparing for the kingdom of God.

'To another he [Jesus] said, "Follow me." But he said, "Lord, let me first go and bury my father." But he said to him, "Leave the dead to bury their own dead; but as for you, go and proclaim the kingdom of God." Another said, "I will follow you, Lord; but let me first say farewell to those at my home." Jesus said to him, "No one who puts his hand to the plough and looks back is fit for the kingdom of God"' (Luke 9.59–62).

The demand is for immediate self-surrender to the cause of the kingdom and the rejection of all temporal concerns.

There was extreme urgency in Jesus' teaching. Individuals had to act immediately to be part of the kingdom of God. Time had run out for men to strive to gradually establish a more perfect society on earth. A rich man had a bountiful harvest and decided to build larger barns to store the grain for his use in years to come. God said to him, 'Fool! This night your soul is required of you; and the things you have prepared, whose will they be?' (Luke 12.16–21). In the context of imminent change as preached by Jesus, such projects were futile and irrelevant.

This rejection of earthly preoccupations implies that poverty is an essential requisite for entry into the kingdom.

A young man asked Jesus, 'What good deed must I do to have eternal life?'

Jesus responds, 'If you would enter life, keep the commandment.'

He responded, 'All these I have observed; what do I still lack?'

Jesus said to him 'If you would be perfect, go, sell what you possess and give to the poor, and you will have treasure in heaven; and come, follow me.'

When the young man heard this he went away sorrowful; for he had great possessions. And Jesus said to his disciples, 'Truly, I say to you, it will be hard for a rich man to enter the kingdom of heaven. Again I tell you, it is easier for a camel to go through the eye of a needle than for a rich man to enter the kingdom of God' (Matthew 19.16–24; Mark 10.17–25; Luke 18.18–25).

Jesus uses hyperbole to emphasise the message. In the first of the beatitudes, Jesus says, 'Blessed are you poor, for yours is the kingdom of God.' (Luke 6.20) Matthew qualifies the statement by inserting 'in spirit'.

'Blessed are the poor in spirit, for theirs is the kingdom of heaven.' (Matthew 5.3) Matthew places the emphasis on humility.

Individual acts of charity to fellow human beings were key essentials to enter the kingdom of God:

I was hungry and you gave me food,
I was thirst and you gave me drink,
I was a stranger and you welcomed me,
I was naked and you clothed me,
I was sick and you visited me,
I was in prison and you came to me (Matthew 25.35–36).

The Synoptic Gospels say very little about the nature of the kingdom of God and what they say is couched in parables. The kingdom of God is present here and now in a latent form that will become manifest. In the parable of the sower, seed is scattered on the path, on rocky ground and amongst thorns, all of which fail to grow. Other seeds fell onto good ground and thrived. The emphasis here is not on the sower, who does not appear particularly competent but on the providential relationship between the seed [preaching] and the good soil [the reaction of the listener] (Mark 4.3–9). The kingdom of God is like a mustard seed, the smallest of seeds that grows to be the largest of shrubs. The kingdom of God has insignificant beginnings but will grow beyond all expectations (Mark 4.30–32). The parable of the leaven in which a small quantity of yeast imperceptibly results in a large quantity of bread echoes the same message (Matthew 13.33).

Jesus stresses the immanency of the kingdom:

Truly, I say to you, there are some standing here who will not taste death before they see the kingdom of God come with power (Mark 9.1; Luke 9.27).

Matthew modifies the teaching with, 'Who will not taste death before they see the Son of man coming in his kingdom', thereby introducing the concept of Jesus' second coming (Matthew 16.28). The whole ethos of Jesus' teaching is dominated by the concept that 'The kingdom of God is at hand' (Mark 1.15).

Several parables stress the need for continuous vigilance. The parable of the doorkeeper who has to be on watch whilst his master is away but is fearful that his master will return when he is asleep, 'for you do not know when the time will come' appears in all three gospels (Mark 13.33–37). The parable of the ten virgins describes how they went to meet a bridegroom but he was delayed and they fell asleep. On his arrival five of the virgins had spare oil for their lamps and went into the marriage feast. The other five were not prepared and had to go to buy oil. When they returned the door was closed and they were refused admission (Matthew 25.1–13).

We return to the question as to why Jesus says so little about the nature of the kingdom of God. Nearly all his teaching is about preparation for the kingdom, emphasising man's moral response. His audience was familiar with the concept of the kingdom of God and there was no reason for him to reiterate what they already knew. Just as they had been delivered from Egypt, God would intervene again decisively and change the world order as predicted by so many of their prophets. Neither John the Baptist or Jesus would have had any impact on the Jews except that they were reiterating their deeply held hopes and aspirations that were reflected in various forms throughout the TaNaKh. Even after the destruction of the Temple in 70 AD, every Sabbath in the synagogue they would say the Jewish prayer, the Quaddish, 'May he establish his kingdom in your life and in your days and in the life of all the house of Israel, speedily and in a short time' (quoted in Vermes 1993 p. 134). Jesus' mission had to make sense to his contemporary first-century Jewish hearers. I draw an analogy to emphasise the point. On 28 August 1965 at the Lincoln Memorial in Washington, Martin Luther King delivered his "I have a dream speech", one of the most influential speeches of the twentieth century. In it he quotes from the United States Declaration of Independence and from the Old Testament, particularly the Psalms, Isaiah and Amos. All these quotations would have been familiar to most of his audience, hence its impact. Supposing we think of another subjugated people such as the Tibetans; had Martin Luther King delivered a similar speech there it would have made no impact as their culture is so different. Jesus was addressing an audience in terms that were intelligible to them.

The Kingdom of God and the Gentile World

Jesus saw his mission as exclusively to the Jews: 'I was sent only to the lost sheep of the house of Israel' (Matt. 15.24). Jesus instructed his disciples to:

'Go nowhere among the Gentiles, and enter no town of the Samaritans, but go rather to the lost sheep of the house of Israel. And preach as you go, saying, "The kingdom of heaven is at hand". Heal the sick, raise the dead, cleanse lepers and cast out demons' (Matthew 10.5–8).

It is with great reluctance that Jesus casts out a demon from the daughter of a Syrophoenician woman with the statement, 'Let the children first be fed, for it is not right to take the children's bread and throw it to the dogs' (Matt. 15.21–28; Mark 7.24–30). Jewish children take precedence over Gentiles

115

sarcastically referred to as dogs. Again he repeats his message, 'Do not give dogs what is holy; and do not throw your pearls before swine' (Matt. 7.6).

On the other hand, Jesus is quoted as saying, 'Go therefore and make disciples of all nations, baptizing them in the name of the Father and of the Son and of the Holy Spirit' (Matthew 28.19; Mark 16.15–16). Luke's gospel concludes:

Thus it is written, that Christ should suffer and on the third day rise from the dead, and that repentance and forgiveness of sins should be preached in his name to all nations (24.46–47).

Matthew incorporates the same sentiment in Jesus' last sermon prior to his crucifixion, 'And this gospel of the kingdom will be preached throughout the whole world, as a testimony to all nations; and then the end will come' (Matthew 24.14).

Faced with such contradictory views that cannot be reconciled we are obliged to choose based on the evidence. During his lifetime, Jesus' activities were almost exclusively with the Jews and reflected Jewish beliefs. Jesus' reference to Gentiles as dogs or swine would have been an embarrassment to the primitive Gentile church and it is inconceivable that the authors would have invented such statements. These were teachings of Jesus that had been handed down reflecting the exclusive nature of the Jewish community. This is illustrated in the early history of the Jewish followers of Jesus who after his death continued to observe the Torah. They worshiped in the Temple (Luke 24.53; Acts 3.1; 5.12, 42; 21.26; 22.17) whilst awaiting the kingdom of God. At first no Gentile could be admitted to the Christian community without first becoming a fully fledged proselyte to the Jewish fold (Acts 10–11). It was with great difficulty that Paul and Barnabas persuaded the leaders of the Christian community in Jerusalem that Gentiles should not be obliged to undergo circumcision or observe the whole of the Law of Moses (Acts 15). At no point was Jesus' command that, 'this gospel of the kingdom will be preached throughout the whole world' entered into the debate regarding the admission of Gentiles. In particular, when Paul met Peter and James in Jerusalem c. 42 and 49 AD the two disciples were clearly unaware of Jesus' command to preach the gospel to the whole world. Such a statement must be regarded as an editorial addition in the light of changed circumstances with the destruction of the Temple and the majority of Jews having rejected Jesus as Messiah. What is most incongruous is the instruction to 'baptize them in the name of the Father and of the Son and of the Holy Spirit'. Such a sophisticated Christological formula was absent from Jesus' earlier teaching and reflects a development in the early church after his death. Such a command could not be an authentic saying of Jesus.

John's Gospel makes only one reference to the kingdom of God. Jesus says to Nicodemus, a high ranking Pharisee, 'Truly, truly, I say to you, unless one is born anew, he cannot see the kingdom of God' (John 3.3). From John's perspective the kingdom of God as perceived in the Old Testament and by Jesus' contemporaries was fading. John was writing about seventy years after the crucifixion of Jesus and thirty years after the destruction of the Temple. His audience was predominantly Gentile following the split with the Jews who followed Jesus. In the Synoptic Gospels, Jesus' teaching is mainly concerned with God as the heavenly father, the imminent arrival of the kingdom of God, and the religious and moral obligations on the people to enter the kingdom of God through repentance. With John's theological concept of Jesus as the Word or Logos (see chapter 12 of the present work) there is a radical change in the portrayal of Jesus. In contrast to the Synoptic Gospels John's account of the teaching of Jesus is focussed on Jesus himself, his person, his teaching and his personal relationship to God and to those who believed in him.

A few examples may suffice:

'You are from below, I am from above; you are of this world, I am not of this world' (John 8.23).
'I came from the Father and have come into the world; again, I am leaving the world and going to the Father' (John 16.28).

For God so loved the world that he gave his only Son, that whoever believes in him should not perish but have eternal life. For God sent the Son into the world, not to condemn the world, but that the world might be saved through him (John 3.16–17).

He who believes in the Son has eternal life; he who does not obey the Son shall not see life, but the wrath of God rests upon him (John 3.36).

The glory which thou hast given me I have given to them, that they may be one even as we are one, I in them and thou in me, that they may become perfectly one, so that the world may know that thou hast sent me and hast loved them even as thou hast loved me (John 17.22–23).

Jesus said to him:

'Have I been with you so long, and yet you do not know me, Phillip? He who has seen me has seen the Father; how can you say, "Show me the Father"? Do you not believe that I am in the Father and the Father in me? The words that I say to you I do not speak on my own authority; but the Father who dwells in me does his works' (John 14.9–10).

'I am the bread of life; he who comes to me shall not hunger, and he who believes in me shall not thirst' (John 6.35).

'I am the way, and the truth, and the life; no one comes to the Father, but by me' (John 14.6).

In conclusion, the Synoptic Gospels portray Jesus essentially as the messenger proclaiming the kingdom of God in terms that resonated with Hebrew scriptures. In John's gospel, Jesus is almost elevated to divine status and equality with God when he says, 'I and the Father are one' (John 10.30). On the other hand, Jesus admits that, 'I go to the Father; as the Father is greater than

I' (John 14.28). The New Testament reflects an evolving construction of Jesus' significance.

We should not underestimate the enduring power of the belief in the kingdom of God. Even after the destruction of the Temple, the messianic hope remains in the fundamental Jewish prayer known as the Eighteen Benedictions, its present form probably redacted between 70 and 100 AD:

> Proclaim our liberation with the great trumpet, raise a banner to gather together our dispersed, assemble us from the four corners of the earth. Blessed are you, Lord, who gathers the banished of your people Israel... And to your city, Jerusalem, return with mercy and dwell in its midst as you have spoken; build it up soon in our days to be an everlasting building, and raise it up quickly in its midst the throne of David. Blessed are you, Lord, who builds Jerusalem. Cause the shoot of David to shoot forth quickly, and raise up the horn of his salvation... bring back the worship into the Holy of Holies in your house. Blessed are you, Lord, who causes your presence to return to Zion (Quoted in Fredriksen 1999 p.247).

Perhaps more pertinent is Israel's national anthem which reflects their continuing expectation:

> As long as in the heart, within,
> A Jewish soul still yearns,
> And onward, towards the ends of the East,
> An eye still gazes towards Zion;
> Our hope is not yet lost,
> The hope of two thousand years,
> To be a free people in our land,
> The land of Zion and Jerusalem.

Up to this point the cardinal message of the Synoptic Gospels was that Jesus endorsed Mosaic Law and urged the people to prepare for the imminent arrival of the kingdom of God when the Jewish nation would be vindicated. Subsequent events would profoundly influence the formulation of Christian belief.

VIII

Jesus' Last Week in Jerusalem

Jesus, his disciples and others went to Jerusalem for the festival of Pesach or Passover. This was a busy time in Jerusalem as vast numbers of pilgrims would be there. There are no reliable figures but it is thought that several hundred thousand were present. Some would stay in Jerusalem, others in neighbouring villages and the remainder in tents or booths. Law and order was primarily the responsibility of the high priest, in this instance Caiaphas, supported by the Temple guards. For major festivals the Roman prefect, Pontius Pilate, would go from his palace in Caesarea to be resident in Jerusalem with up to three thousand soldiers. They would watch proceedings from the parapet on the outer walls of the Temple.

Passover was always held on the fifteenth day of Nisan (Lev. 23.5). Nisan was the first month of the Jewish calendar and corresponds to the end of March and beginning of April in the Gregorian calendar. Our dates change at midnight whereas the Jewish date changed at sunset, about six p.m. our time. This is relevant when we consider Jesus' Last Supper. The rules concerning Passover are detailed in Exodus chapter 12. Pilgrims arrived in Jerusalem by the 8th Nisan to undergo ritual purification by bathing in the special pools or *mikvahs* and being sprinkled with the ash of a sacrificed red heifer. Purification did not imply any moral censure but was a means of removing impurities such as contact with a corpse, menstrual blood or giving birth. These regulations were set down in the Torah (Numbers 19) and were a prerequisite for entry into the Temple. There is no mention of Jesus and his disciples undergoing ritual purification but as this was universally accepted practice by the Jews its mention would be superfluous. An unblemished male lamb or goat would be selected on the 10th Nisan and ritually slaughtered on the 14th Nisan. It would be roasted that night, after six p.m. on the 15th. Nisan and eaten with unleavened bread and bitter herbs. Any lamb remaining was destroyed by burning before sunrise. The feast of unleavened bread continued for another seven or eight days.

As Jesus approaches Jerusalem he instructs his disciples to acquire an ass on which he rides into the city. John's Gospel (12.14) quotes Zechariah (9.9), 'Fear not, daughter of Zion; behold thy king is coming, sitting on an ass's colt!' He is greeted by large numbers of pilgrims. Of crucial importance to subsequent events was the crowd hailing Jesus the son of David hence 'Messiah' (Matthew 21.9) and 'King' (Luke 19.38; John 12.13).

> And those who went before and those who followed cried out, 'Hosanna! Blessed be he who comes in the name of the Lord! Blessed be the kingdom of our father David that is coming! Hosanna in the highest!' (Mark 11.9–10).

What did the crowd expect of Jesus, particularly those who were relatively new to his mission? He would have been regarded as a charismatic person, a prophet, and a miracle worker who spoke of the imminent kingdom of God. In the politically charged environment their hope must have been for a Davidic King Messiah and that Jesus would take the royal throne of David, lead the Jews and vanquish the Romans.

Josephus, in describing the cause of the rebellion that led to the destruction of the Temple captures the atmosphere that would have existed to some extent at the time of Jesus:

> ...an ambiguous oracle, likewise found in their sacred scriptures, to the effect that at that time one from their country would become ruler of the world. This they understood to be one of their own race and many of their wise men went astray in their interpretation of it. The oracle,

however, in reality signified the sovereignty of Vespasian, who was proclaimed emperor on Jewish soil (Josephus, *Wars* 6:5:4).

Jesus had not been regarded as the Messiah in Galilee. The disciples did not initiate this adulation. It must have been other pilgrims encountering Jesus possibly for the first time. As Jesus continued to teach in the Temple area it is probable that the crowd became more excited as the feast approached. For the authorities this was a tinderbox situation.

Jesus and the Temple Authorities

On the following day, Jesus:

> ...entered the Temple and began to drive out those who sold and those who bought in the Temple, and he overturned the tables of the money-changers and the seats of those who sold pigeons (Mark 11.15).

He commented, 'My house shall be called a house of prayer, but you have made it a den of robbers.' These are phrases from Isaiah (56.7) and Jeremiah (7.11). The pilgrims from all parts of the Mediterranean would arrive with various currencies. These had to be converted into silver drachms minted in Tyre, the only coins deemed suitable for sacred donations. The silver content of these drachms was assured but perhaps more importantly did not bear any offensive images such as the head of another country. The availability of unblemished animals at the Temple was an essential service for the pilgrims.

Jesus' gesture has been regarded by many of being symbolic acts indicating either reform of Temple practices or the destruction of the Temple. There is no evidence in the gospels that he wished to reform the large and complex Temple system. The Temple was central to Judaism and an attack on it would represent an attack on the whole way of life of the Jews. Jesus endorses Temple practise by emphasising the importance of settling disputes prior to offering sacrifice (Matthew 5.23–24).

Even after Jesus' death, his disciples continue to worship and offer sacrifices in the Temple (Acts 2.46; 3.1; 5.12, 42; 21.23–26). Jesus appears to predict the destruction of the Temple:

> And as he came out of the Temple, one of his disciples said to him, 'Look, Teacher, what wonderful stones and what wonderful buildings!' and Jesus said to him, 'Do you see these great buildings? There will not be left here one stone upon another, that will not be thrown down' (Mark 13.1–2).

Both Matthew (24.1–2) and Luke (21.5–6) reiterate the account with minor variations. At Jesus' trial he is charged for saying, 'I will destroy this Temple that is made with hands, and in three days I will build another, not made with hands'(Mark 14.57–59). The witnesses were in disagreement. The implication is that Jesus did not threaten to destroy the Temple. Paul, writing about the coming Kingdom, never mentions Jesus' prophesy. This raises the question as whether or not Jesus actually said these words or where they editorial additions after the event – the destruction of the Temple in 70 AD. The dating of Mark's gospel remains a contentious issue although most date it after 70 AD.

Jesus' background was rural Galilee and he could have been shocked by the vast crowds, noise and the bargaining at the Temple. He would have expected a more orderly and dignified approach to the necessary commercial transactions within the Temple complex. The commotion he created would have alarmed the Temple authorities.

John's account is rather different. In the Synoptic Gospels, Jesus and his disciples go to Jerusalem for only one Passover feast. In John they attend on three separate occasions (2.13; 6.4; 11.55) thus extending his ministry over three years. It was only on his first visit to the Temple that Jesus overturned the tables. This could not have been the reason for his arrest three years later. The authorities would have been aware of Jesus' teaching which did not constitute a direct threat to them or Rome. The threat to law and order came from the expectant and enthusiastic crowds. According to John it was the raising of Lazarus from the dead and Jesus' reputation for 'performing many signs' that concerned the Temple authorities. As has already been discussed, the Synoptic Gospels make no reference to Lazarus.

> The following day a deputation representing the chief priests, scribes and elders approached Jesus in the Temple.
> And they said to him, 'By what authority are you doing these things, or who gave you this authority to do them?'
> Jesus said to them, 'I will ask you a question; answer me and I will tell you by what authority I do these things. Was the baptism of John from heaven or from men? Answer me.'
> And they argued with one another. 'If we say from heaven he will say, why then did you not believe him? But shall we say from men?' – They were afraid of the people, for all held that John was a real prophet. So they answered Jesus, 'We do not know.'
> And Jesus said to them, 'Neither will I tell you by what authority I do these things' (Matthew 21.23–7; Mark 11.27–33; Luke 20.1–8).

The questioning referred to the disturbance in the Temple the previous day. In his response Jesus had outwitted them completely and this would not have gone unnoticed by those standing around and listening. The demoralised deputation would want revenge.

Jesus continued to teach extensively in the Temple, often in response to awkward questions posed by officials:

> In the daytime he would be in the Temple teaching, but would spend the night on the hill called the Mount of Olives. And from early morning the people would gather round him in the Temple to listen to him (Luke 21.37–38).

The officials were becoming increasingly concerned that Jesus' teaching concerning the imminent kingdom of God would incite the crowd's expectations. Two days before Passover, on the 13th Nisan:

The chief priests and the elders of the people gathered in the palace of the high priest, who was called Caiaphas, and took counsel together in order to arrest Jesus by stealth and kill him. But they said, 'Not during the feast, lest there be a tumult among the people' (Matthew 26.3–5; Mark 14.1–2; Luke 22.2).

John's account differs. As Passover approached there was speculation as whether or not Jesus would attend. 'Now the chief priests and the Pharisees had given orders that if anyone knew where he was, he should let them know, so they might arrest him' (John 11.57). The Temple authorities were concerned that the crowds would get out of control and the Roman soldiers would intervene brutally.

Jesus' Last Supper

The Synoptic Gospels describe the disciples going to the Temple to sacrifice the Passover lamb and then finding 'a large upper room furnished and ready' where they celebrated the Passover supper (Mark 14.15). John's Gospel is symbolically different as it places Jesus' last supper 'before the feast of the Passover' (13.1). When Judas left the last supper, some of the disciples thought that he was going 'to buy what we need for the feast' (John 13.29). Later at his trial Jesus is taken early in the morning from Caiaphas' house to Pilate at the praetorium. Those escorting Jesus 'did not enter the praetorium, so that they might not be defiled, but might eat the Passover' (John 18.28). Jesus' last meal may not have been the Jewish *seder* or Passover meal. Subsequent events may help to clarify the discrepancy.

The breaking of bread and after the meal sharing a final drink was not invented by Jesus but was part of the Jewish Passover meal. The head of the family or host took the unleavened bread in his hands and said the *berakah* or thanksgiving then would break the bread, eat a fragment himself and then distribute it to the others. After the meal of roast lamb came the fourth and final cup of wine, known as the cup of blessing or *kos shel berakah*. This remains part of traditional Passover meal.

The Synoptic Gospels give similar accounts of the last supper:

> And as they were eating, he took bread, and blessed, and broke it, and gave it to them, and said, 'Take, this is my body.' And he took a cup, and when he had given thanks he gave it to them, and they all drank of it. And he said to them, 'This is my blood of the covenant, which is poured out for many. Truly, I say to you, I shall not drink again of the fruit of the vine until that day when I drink it new in the kingdom of God' (Mark 14.22–25).

This prediction that he would not drink wine before the arrival of the kingdom of God could be interpreted that he would continue to teach and heal for a short while before God intervened and established his kingdom. Then it would have made no sense for Luke to include the command to, 'Do this in remembrance of me' (Luke 22.20). On the other hand he may have foreseen his impending death. If this were the case then we have difficulty in believing that he thought of himself as the paschal lamb replacing Temple sacrifice and it does not feature in his earlier teaching. This concept appears only after his death and resurrection but became the view of the early Gentile church. His disciples continued to worship in the Temple.

The authors of the New Testament are formulating a theological meaning for his unexpected death. Paul, writing in the early fifties, believed that Jesus' last supper was the Jewish Passover meal. He develops the theme of the Jewish festival of liberation to the advent of the kingdom of God. 'For Christ, our paschal lamb has been sacrificed' (1 Cor. 5.7). The concept is reiterated later in Mark 'For the Son of man also came not to be served but to serve, and to give his life as a ransom for many' (Mark 10.45). The analogy with Jewish sacrifice permeates the New Testament, thus:

You know that you were ransomed from the futile ways inherited from your fathers, not with perishable things such as silver and gold, but with the precious blood of Christ, like that of a lamb without blemish or spot (1 Peter 1.18).

The early church gradually ceased to celebrate the Lord's Supper as a meal but continued the sacrament of breaking bread and sharing wine. Ignatius (c. 115 AD) is credited with giving it the name Eucharist or 'thanksgiving'.

John's account is different. Jesus has supper with his disciples 'before the feast of the Passover' (13.1). Consequently, unlike the Synoptic Gospels, John does not ascribe any special meaning to the meal. Judas departs during the supper. Jesus then washes the disciples' feet as an example of humility. Jesus then enters into a long discourse included in chapters thirteen to seventeen. Jesus anticipates his betrayal, says farewell to his disciples, describes himself as the true vine and the disciples the branches, prepares them to face a hostile world and finally ends with a prayer for the disciples.

All the accounts describe how after supper the whole group went from Jerusalem to an orchard known as Gethsemane on the Mount of Olives.

Betrayal by Judas

Caiaphas was an astute high priest and was responsible for maintaining law and order. He was appointed by the Romans and served for eighteen years, ten of them being directly answerable to Pontius Pilate. He was anxious that the crowds should not get out of control in their adulation of Jesus. The chief priests could not believe how their fortune had changed and their opportunity had come:

Then Judas Iscariot, who was one of the twelve, went to the chief priests in order to betray him to them. And when they heard it they were glad, and promised to give him money. And he sought an opportunity to betray him (Mark 14.10–11; Matthew 26.14–16; Luke 22.3–6).

Matthew says that Judas demanded that they paid him thirty pieces of silver, apparently the price of the cheapest slave. What was Judas' motive? It is difficult to believe that one of Jesus' disciples, with all that Jesus had said about material wealth, could have been motivated by greed. The money could well have been an unsolicited gift that he later returned. Luke simply blames Satan, a mindless evil act (22.3). Some have tried to rehabilitate Judas by suggesting that he was doing the will of God. Certainly without the crucifixion of Jesus, Christianity as we know it would not have existed. Judas however could not have anticipated such an outcome. When Jesus was condemned Judas committed suicide (Matt. 27.5). Perhaps Judas was an impatient man and was anxious that the kingdom of God be established immediately. Passover would be an appropriate symbolic moment and a confrontation between the elders and Jesus should precipitate God's intervention. Judas' motivation remains a mystery.

Arrest and Trial of Jesus

In the orchard known as Gethsemane on the Mount of Olives Jesus left his disciples to pray alone 'Abba, Father, all things are possible to thee; remove this cup from me; yet not what I will, but what thou wilt' (Mark 14.36; Matthew 26.39; Luke 22.42). The cup is a symbol of tragic destiny. Meanwhile the disciples slept. They are disturbed by 'a crowd with swords and clubs' led by Judas (Mark 14.43). According to the Synoptic Gospels the arresting party consisted of chief priests, scribes and elders, although John includes 'a band of soldiers and their captain' (18.12) indicating Roman involvement in the arrest. If this was the case then Caiaphas must have told Pilate of his intention to arrest Jesus. Pilate would have volunteered some of his soldiers to ensure that the arrest went ahead as expeditiously as possible. In other words they had already decided that Jesus should at least be taken out of circulation.

Simon Peter puts up a token resistance and cuts off the right ear of the high priest's slave. According to John he was called Malchus. In all four accounts Jesus tells Simon Peter to 'Put your sword back into its place; for all who take the sword will perish by the sword' (Matthew 26.52). Only Luke recounts Jesus healing the slave's ear (22.51). Jesus offers no resistance with the following words:

> 'Have you come out as against a robber, with swords and clubs to capture me? Day after day I was with you in the Temple teaching and you did not seize me. But let the scriptures be fulfilled' (Mark 14.49).

At this point all the disciples fled. They were not thought to be a threat to law and order in Jerusalem or they would also have been arrested.

Simon Peter then surreptitiously follows the arresting party to the courtyard of the high priest. As he warmed himself by a fire a maid of the high priest said, 'You also were with the Nazarene, Jesus', but he denied it. She challenged him again at the gateway but he denied any knowledge of Jesus. Later bystanders challenged him again, no doubt because of his dialectal Aramaic, characteristic of Galileans. He refuted the charge but as a cock crowed for the second time, he remembered Jesus' prediction that he would deny him three times (Matthew 26.57–58; 69–75; Mark 14.53–54; 66–72; Luke 22.54).

The gospels contain contradictory accounts of Jesus' trial. Matthew (26.57–68) closely follows that of Mark (14.53–65). Jesus is taken to the high priest, Caiaphas. Already present were the chief priests, elders and scribes, representing the Sanhedrin or high court. In essence, the court seeks incriminating testimony, many false witnesses perjure themselves and Jesus remains silent. Finally, maybe out of desperation Caiaphas demands, 'Are you the Christ, the son of God?' In Matthew his response is, 'You have said so.' The response is typical of the indirect way Jesus refers to himself and can be interpreted as either yes or no. In Rabbinic literature however the understanding would be 'You, not I' meaning I would disagree, or at least would not put it that way. In Mark we have a direct 'I am' although other Mark manuscripts give Matthew's response. Jesus then goes on to speak of the exalted Son of Man. The court

130

deems this blasphemous whereupon the guards mock Jesus and abuse him.

That the whole council and witnesses were present presupposes that Caiaphas was certain that Jesus would be arrested that night. It would not have been easy to convene such a court at short notice and very late at night. As the sun set they would return to their families to roast their lamb and enjoy the Passover feast with the traditional four cups of wine. Convening the Sanhedrin that night without prior warning would have been almost impossible.

More importantly, the trial as described did not conform to Mosaic Law. From the ninth century BC the law was administered locally.

> You shall appoint judges and officers in all the towns which the Lord your God gives you, according to your tribes; and they shall judge the people with righteous judgment (Deut. 16.18).

Further:

> If any case arises requiring decision between one case of homicide and another... any case within your towns which is too difficult for you, then you shall arise and go up to the place which the Lord your God will choose, and coming to the Levitical priests, and to the judge who is in office in those days, you shall consult with them, and they shall declare to you the decision (Deut. 17.8).

It was this court, the Sanhedrin, that tried Jesus. The hearing was held in Caiaphas' house rather than the special hall situated in the Temple area, the Hall of the Hewn Stone. Whilst all work was prohibited on the Sabbath (Exodus 31.15) the rule also applied to Feast Days and was the practice in Rabbinical times. Before a person could be sentenced to death reliable witnesses had to give evidence 'On the evidence of two witnesses or of three witnesses he that is to die shall be put to death; a person shall not be put to death on the evidence of one witness' (Deut.

17.6). The witness was obliged to throw the first stone. Caiaphas concludes the trial, 'He has uttered blasphemy. Why do we still need witnesses?' (Matthew 26.65) This contravened Mosaic Law.

The accusation against Jesus was that of blasphemy as he was described as the Son of God (Matthew 26.63). Jesus' response was, 'You have said so.' This title will be discussed in chapter twelve of the present work. Suffice to say that the title was widely used with different connotations in the Old Testament. To take one example, 'Be like a father to orphans, and as good as a husband to widows. And you will be like a son to the Most High, whose love for you will surpass your mother's' (Ecclesiasticus. 4.10–11 JB). The charge of blasphemy as construed had no basis in biblical law. Matthew and Mark's account of the night trial of Jesus on the 15th of Nissan lacks any credible historical basis.

Luke (22.63; 23.1) makes no mention of the night trial only that the guards mocked Jesus. Luke probably believed that trials conducted at night were illegal according to Jewish law as was the case in the early Rabbinic period. This is reflected later in Luke's account of the trial of Peter and John by the Sanhedrin: 'And they arrested them and put them in custody until the morrow, for it was already evening' (Acts 4.3). The following morning, the 15th Nisan, the Sanhedrin question Jesus along the lines described by Matthew and Mark with evasive answers from Jesus which are considered a confession of guilt but no sentence is passed. The Synoptic Gospels date the trial on the holiest day of the year, Passover. This lacks any historical credibility.

John (18.12–14; 19–24) depicts Jesus being taken from the Garden of Gethsemane not to Caiaphas but to Annas. He had been high priest from 6 to 15 AD and his opinion was highly respected. It would be reasonable to surmise that Caiaphas had asked Annas for his opinion. Caiaphas believed Jesus was a potential threat to his maintaining peace and order during the festival with the further risk of vicious Roman intervention. He hoped that Annas would find incriminating evidence. Jesus' main defence was that he had been teaching openly in the Temple and had nothing to hide. Annas' opinion is not recorded but Jesus is sent bound to Caiaphas who then acted promptly. 'It was Caiaphas who had given counsel to the Jews that it was expedient that one man should die for the people' (John 18.14). John adds his own explanation:

He [Caiaphas] did not say this of his own accord, but being high priest that year he prophesied that Jesus should die for the nation, and not for the nation only, but to gather into one the children of God who are scattered abroad (11.51–52).

This could not have been Caiaphas' motivation in condemning Jesus to death. He simply wished to have Jesus taken out of circulation but to hand over a fellow Jew to a Roman prefect could not have been an easy decision for Caiaphas hence his request for the opinion of Annas.

All four accounts describe Jesus being taken early in the morning to Pilate at the praetorium. John, as mentioned earlier, times the event prior to the Passover meal (18.28). It is noteworthy that up to this point the accusation against Jesus was that of blasphemy as he was described as the Son of God (Matthew 26.63). Pilate would have had no interest in religious arguments between the Jews as he probably regarded them as primitive and superstitious.

The charges are suddenly changed to that of sedition. Pilate questions Jesus, 'Are you King of the Jews?' (Matthew 27.11; Mark 15.2) Luke is more specific, 'We found this man perverting our nation, and forbidding us to give tribute to Caesar, and saying that he himself is Christ the king' (23.2). This was clearly a false accusation. Jesus responds with the evasive answer, 'You have said so'. To further accusations, Jesus fails to respond. Pilate concludes, 'I find no crime in this man'. Luke is unique in recording that Pilate sent Jesus to Herod Antipas, governor of Galilee, who was in Jerusalem for the festival. As a native of Nazareth, Jesus would come under his jurisdiction. Herod Antipas 'questioned him at some length' then contemptuously dressed him up before sending him back to Pilate (Luke 23.6–12). Luke describes a very tight schedule for that morning with the Sanhedrin's first meeting, trial by Pilate, examination by Herod, final sentencing by Pilate and Jesus crucified by 'about the sixth hour' (Luke 23.44). This would have been noon in our time.

According to John, Pilate found that Jesus was no threat to Roman interests and says, 'Take him yourselves and judge him by your own law.'

They responded, 'It is not lawful for us to put any man to death' (John 18.31). The implication was that the Romans had removed this right. The traditional penalty for adultery or rape was stoning to death. Romans would not wish to get involved in such details. Notices were placed in the Temple indicating that any Gentile, including Romans, going further than the Gentile court would face a death sentence. After a hearing by the Sanhedrin, for example, Stephen is found guilty of blasphemy and stoned to death (Acts 7.57–60). John tries to explain why Jesus was to die at the hands of the Romans by crucifixion rather than by the Jewish practice of stoning by writing, 'This was to fulfil the word which Jesus had spoken to show by what death he was to die' (John 18.32). There is no evidence to corroborate this but perhaps helps to mitigate the deceit that the Jews had no death penalty.

Only the Synoptic Gospels recall in slightly different ways a custom whereby the governor would release one prisoner during the festival. What is remarkable is that the crowd have the choice of which prisoner to release. They choose Barabbas, 'who had been thrown into prison for an insurrection started in the city, and for murder' (Luke 23:19). Pilate offers to release Jesus but the crowd demanded that Barabbas be released. There is no other record of Barabbas. Furthermore, Josephus describes the history of the Jewish people of that time in minute detail but makes no reference to the release of a prisoner during Passover. It would not have been in Pilate's character to act irresponsibly and allow the crowd to release a murderer.

Mark (15.12–20) describes how Pilate asks, 'Why what evil has he done?' There is no response and Pilate concedes to the will of the people to crucify Jesus. Jesus was then taken into the praetorium and the soldiers 'clothed him in a purple cloak, and plaiting a crown of thorns they put it on him. And they began to salute him, "Hail, King of the Jews!"'

Matthew's account (27.21–31) is identical except that Pilate washes his hands, saying, 'I am innocent of this man's blood, see to it yourselves.' Matthew places the blame on the Jewish people when they say, 'His blood be on us and on our children!' Luke (23.20–24) omits the mocking of Jesus. John (19.1–16) portrays Pilate as first scourging Jesus then presenting him to the crowd in the hope that they would change their minds and feel that he had been punished enough. This was to no avail and Pilate took Jesus into the praetorium to question him again. Again Pilate appeals to the crowd but they cry, 'If you release this man, you are not Caesar's friend; everyone who makes himself a king sets himself against Caesar.'

Pilate said to them, 'Behold your King!'

They responded, 'We have no king but Caesar.'

'Then he handed him over to them [Roman soldiers] to be crucified.' The Gospel accounts were aimed at the Gentile inhabitants of the Greek-speaking world. Although Jesus was crucified by Pontius Pilate, it was necessary to prove that being a Christian is not incompatible with loyalty to Caesar and the Roman Empire. The actions of Pontius Pilate were glossed over and those of the Jewish leaders and through them the Jewish people at large were denigrated.

The Crucifixion

The synoptic accounts of the crucifixion have one incident in common. The Roman soldiers compelled an otherwise unknown man, Simon of Cyrene, to carry Jesus' cross to Golgotha. As in the nativity narratives, the authors use the *pesher* argument to demonstrate that Jesus, quite literally, died according to the scriptures. Thus, Psalm 69.21, 'and for my thirst they gave me vinegar to drink' and Proverbs 31.6, 'And give strong drink to him who is perishing, and wine to those in bitter distress' appears in Matthew and Mark as, 'And they offered him wine mingled with myrrh'. Psalm 22.18, 'They divide my garments among them, and for my raiment they cast lots' is recorded by

Matthew and Mark as history. It is difficult to conceive of any motive for the soldiers to be interested in Jesus' clothes. Psalm 22.7, 'All who see me mock at me, they wag their heads' becomes, 'And those who passed by derided him, wagging their heads, and saying, "You who would destroy the temple, and build it in three days, save yourself".' Again Psalm 34.20, 'He keeps all his bones; not one of them is broken' and Zechariah 12.10, 'When they look on him whom they have pierced, they shall mourn for him, as one mourns for an only child' are interpreted by John (19.31–37) as relevant facts.

The Jews asked Pilate that their [the two robbers'] legs be broken, and that they may be taken away [breaking their legs meant that they were suspended only by their arms which accelerated death by asphyxiation]. So the soldiers came and broke the legs of the first, and of the other who had been crucified with him; but when they came to Jesus and saw that he was already dead, they did not break his legs. But one of the soldiers pierced his side with a spear, and at once there came out blood and water. He who saw it has borne witness – his testimony is true, and he knows that he tells the truth – that you also may believe. For these things took place that the scripture might be fulfilled, 'Not a bone of him shall be broken'. And again another scripture says, 'They shall look on him whom they have pierced'.

These narratives are steeped in theological overtones dependent on Old Testament prophesy. To what extent we can accept the details as historically true is open to question. All that we can be certain about is that Jesus was crucified soon after his arrest. Pilate had him crucified as a potential insurgent and mockingly places an inscription on the cross 'King of the Jews' (Mark.15.26). John's version (19.19) is, 'Jesus of Nazareth, the King of the Jews' written in Hebrew, Latin and Greek.

Whilst on the cross, Jesus is reported to have uttered a few words. Matthew (47:46, 50) copies Mark's account (15.34–36):

And at the ninth hour Jesus cried with a loud voice,

'Eloi, Eloi, lama sabachthani?' which means, 'My God, my God, why hast thou forsaken me?' ... And Jesus uttered a loud cry, and breathed his last.

This is the first verse of Psalm 22 spoken in Aramaic. It is the only occasion he does not address God as Father. Luke (23.34) uniquely includes the prayer, 'Father, forgive them for they know not what they do'. Within the context of the verse this refers to the Romans thus exonerating them. Luke also records a conversation with one of the robbers crucified with him.

And he said, 'Jesus, remember me when you come in your kingly power.' And he said to him, 'Truly, I say to you, today you will be with me in Paradise' (Luke 23.42–43).

Then Jesus, crying with a loud voice, said, 'Father, into thy hands I commit my spirit!' And having said this he breathed his last (Luke 23.46).

John describes Mary, Jesus' mother, her sister and Mary Magdalene at the foot of the cross. Matthew and Mark describe a group of women, including Mary Magdalene but not Mary, Jesus' mother, standing some distance away. Nevertheless, according to John (19.26–27):

When Jesus saw his mother, and the disciple whom he loved standing near, he said to his mother, 'Woman, behold your son!' Then he said to the disciple, 'Behold your mother!' And from that hour the disciple took her to his own home. Soon afterwards, He said, 'It is finished'; and he bowed his head and gave up his spirit (John 19.30).

Instead of the cry of dereliction in Matthew and Mark, Jesus at the moment of death makes an affirmation that his work is complete.

In the Synoptic Gospels the death of Jesus is associated with cosmic events. There was darkness over the whole land from noon to three p.m., a common element of apocalyptic imagery.

'The curtain in the temple was torn in two, from top to bottom', perhaps signifying the end of Judaism. Mathew refers to an earthquake:

> ... and the rocks were split; the tombs also were opened, and many bodies of the saints who had fallen asleep were raised, and coming out of the tombs after his resurrection they went into the holy city and appeared to many (Matthew 27.52–53).

There is no further mention of these individuals.

In keeping with the general emphasis in the account of Jesus' trial and death, it was appropriate that the first person to recognise the greatness of Jesus was a Gentile and more significantly the Roman centurion in charge of his crucifixion. He said, 'Truly this man is a son of God!' (Matthew 27.54; Mark 15.39) In Luke he said, 'Certainly this man was innocent!' (23.47).

The Burial of Jesus

Soon after the death of Jesus, Joseph of Arimathea asks Pilate for permission to remove the body from the cross. Joseph is variously described as a disciple of Jesus (Matt. 27.57; John 19.38), or a respected member of the Sanhedrin (Mark. 15.42; Luke 23.50). Pilate consents to his request. Only in Mark does Pilate first request confirmation of his death from the centurion (15.44–45). Jesus' body is wrapped in a linen shroud and laid in a newly hewn rock tomb. Matthew and Mark describe a great stone being rolled in front of the door of the tomb. John adds that Joseph is assisted by Nicodemus bringing a mixture of myrrh and aloes weighing about one hundred pounds (19.39). This seems rather excessive. In the Synoptic Gospels Mary Magdalene and another Mary or possibly Galilean women watched Joseph of Arimathea at the tomb. Matthew adds that the chief priests ask Pilate to send sentries to guard the tomb for fear that the disciples will steal the body and fake a resurrection. Pilate tells them to use their own soldiers which they do

(Matthew 27.62–66). This may have been an afterthought by Matthew to reduce speculation concerning the fate of Jesus' body.

Some Possible Conclusions

The trial of Jesus as recorded in the four Gospels, leaves us with a confused and at times contradictory picture. It is helpful to first consider Caiaphas' position. It was his responsibility to maintain law and order in Jerusalem. Passover was always a tense time, hence the presence of Pilate and some three thousand soldiers. On this occasion passions were running particularly high. There had been a disturbance in the Temple when Jesus overturned the money lenders' tables. Jesus had been preaching the imminent arrival of the kingdom of God and perhaps some were expecting it at that Passover. Some of the crowd had hailed Jesus as Messiah. Caiaphas was concerned that if the crowds got out of control then the Roman soldiers would intervene, with severe casualties. Pilate had already intervened when there was a large demonstration objecting to the appropriation of Temple funds to the building of a new aqueduct to Jerusalem with considerable loss of life. If trouble broke out, Caiaphas would lose his post. His only option was to remove Jesus from the scene. This was made easier with the help of Judas. Jesus was arrested late at night, away from the crowds with only the disciples present.

Caiaphas' options were very limited. Both Matthew and Mark describe a night trial before the Sanhedrin. The practical difficulties in convening such a meeting after the Passover meal have been discussed. It would be highly irregular and probably illegal to hold a trial at night. More importantly, according to Mosaic Law, the Sanhedrin was prohibited from convening on a Sabbath and by implication on feast days. According to Matthew and Mark, Jesus is taken to Caiaphas's house and not to the council chambers where the Sanhedrin would normally convene. Caiaphas acts as both prosecutor and judge. The trial, as described in the Synoptic Gospels, 'is a travesty of Mosaic Law'. A conviction could not be obtained solely on the confession of

139

the accused. It is worth comparing this trial with that of the apostles a few years later. The apostles had been charged with teaching in the name of Jesus outside the Temple. Luke describes the trial:

When they heard this they were enraged and wanted to kill them. But a Pharisee in the council named Gamaliel, a teacher of the law, held in honour by all the people, stood up and ordered the men to be put outside for a while. And he said to them:

'Men of Israel, take care what you do with these men. For before these days Theudas arose, giving himself out to be somebody, and a number of men, about four hundred joined him; but he was slain and all who followed him were dispersed and came to nothing. After him Judas the Galilean arose in the days of the census and drew away some of the people after him; he also perished, and all who followed were scattered. So in the present case I tell you, keep away from these men and let them alone; for if this plan or this undertaking is of men, it will fail; but if it is of God, you will not be able to overthrow them. You might even be found opposing God!' (Acts 5.33–39).

Just suppose that the Sanhedrin had delivered a guilty verdict on the charge of blasphemy then the sentence would have been stoning to death in public. Would this not have caused further unrest? Caiaphas had the legal right to condemn Jesus to death but the practicalities of carrying it out made this an impossible choice. Caiaphas undertook his duties with considerable skill and would have considered his options carefully.

The gospels all portray Pilate as a considerate and sympathetic figure doing his utmost to avoid being culpable for Jesus' crucifixion. All four accounts were written after the uprising by the Jews against Roman occupation culminating in the destruction of Jerusalem in 70 AD. This had been a horrendous war involving Rome's most experienced general, Vespasian. It was imperative that the Christian movement reassured the Gentiles that they neither challenged nor threatened the Roman empire as the Jews had. It was the Jews, not Pilate, who were responsible for Jesus' death. In the Synoptic Gospels, the trial narratives are construed to place the blame entirely on the Jews. Their accounts lack credence when examined in the light of Jewish practice at the time.

John includes the statement, 'When Pilate heard these words, he was the more afraid' (19.8). This was not the Pilate of history. Philo described him as a man of 'inflexible, cruel disposition', whose administration was marked by his 'venality, thefts, assaults, abusive behaviour and his frequent murders of untried prisoners' (quoted in Fredriksen, 1988, p.79). One of Pilate's last recorded acts was to suppress an uprising in Samaria in 36AD, with such brutality that the Roman governor of Syria, Vitellius, sent him to Rome to explain his actions. His behaviour was unacceptable even to his masters in Rome. The real Pilate was not one to waste time on legal niceties.

John's Gospel is regarded as the most theologically advanced. It would also appear to be as close to a historical account of Jesus' last days as we can reconstruct. There was a meeting of the Sanhedrin to discuss their attitude towards Jesus, not after his arrest, but either before or after his arrival in Jerusalem. They said, 'What are we to do? For this man performs many signs. If we let him go on thus, every one will believe him, and the Romans will come and destroy both our holy place and our nation' (John 11.47–48).

Caiaphas responded:

'You know nothing at all; you do not understand that it is expedient for you that one man should die for the people, and that the whole nation should not perish...' So from that day on they took counsel how to put him to death (John 11.49–53).

Caiaphas would have discussed his predicament with Pilate. Without Pilate's consent there would not have been Roman troops present at the arrest of Jesus. Pilate's response would have been words to the effect, 'Hand him to me and I will see to the rest'. Once Jesus had been arrested, at night and away from the crowds, he was taken to Annas' house for his opinion. He was then taken to Caiaphas who refers him to Pilate. From what we know of Pilate he would not have hesitated for a moment to issue a sentence of death. In the charged atmosphere at the end of the first century with Roman distrust for the Jews, it was imperative that the Gospels should exonerate Pilate and blame the Jews for the death of Jesus. This would explain the account of the release of Barabbas. The latter can only be described as an improbable and totally irresponsible act by Pilate. Nevertheless, it effectively portrays the Jews as demanding the death of Jesus and the release of the murderer, Barabbas.

This scenario may disturb some Christians but it concurs with the account in John's Gospel and corresponds to legal constraints on Caiaphas. Jesus died a few hours before the Passover Feast and much of the Christian symbolism built into the Synoptic Gospels is therefore lost. Caiaphas would have enjoyed his Passover meal that night relieved in the belief that he had quietly and expeditiously removed a potential trouble maker. Another Passover Festival would have been celebrated uneventfully. This was not to be. The consequences of his actions, or more importantly, how they were portrayed in the Synoptic Gospels, permeates society to this day. The roots of anti-Semitism are complex. The Jews were derided by those with Hellenistic beliefs for centuries prior to the birth of Jesus. The Synoptic Gospels attributed the crucifixion of Jesus to the actions of the Jews. This amounted to deicide for many Christians and was used as justification for their persecution of Jews. Christians have a moral responsibility to confront their unquestioning acceptance of the account in the Synoptic Gospels, and its contribution to the centuries of anti-Semitic atrocities.

IX

The Resurrection of Jesus

Jesus was dead and had been laid to rest in the tomb of Joseph of Arimathea. The disciples had fled from the Garden of Gethsemane and that night Peter had thrice denied any knowledge of Jesus. They must have been terrified, thinking that perhaps Caiaphas or Pilate would arrest them next. They would also have been completely disillusioned and demoralised. They had believed that the kingdom of God was at hand, possibly at that Passover. A glorious age where the first would be last and the meek would inherit the earth was not to be. Then, like a bolt from the blue, something unexpected and very strange happened. Perhaps *inexplicable* would be a more appropriate description. Early on the Sunday morning, Mary Magdalene and two other women went to the tomb to anoint Jesus' body but the tomb was empty. Mary then saw an apparition of Jesus, but when she reported this to those who had been with him they did not believe her (Mark 16.1–11).

As there are such differences between the accounts in the four Gospels, they are best considered in the sequence in which they were written, Mark, Matthew, Luke and John.

Mark

Mark gives two accounts. The oldest surviving manuscripts of Mark end at 16.8. Subsequent verses were written in a different style of Greek, indicating that they are by a different author. In the original version, early on Sunday morning Mary Magdalene and two other women go to the tomb to anoint Jesus' body. There they find the stone in front of the entrance had been rolled back. A young man dressed in a white robe told them that Jesus had risen and that they were to tell the disciples that he had gone to Galilee where they would see him, 'And they went out and fled from the tomb; for trembling and astonishment had come upon them; and they said nothing to anyone, for they were afraid' (16.8).

In the extended version, Jesus first appears to Mary Magdalene who reports this to the distressed disciples who do not believe her. Jesus then appears in a different form to two disciples but they were not believed by the others. Jesus then appeared to the eleven disciples as they sat at a table. Jesus gives a final command:

'Go into the world and preach the gospel to the whole creation. He who believes and is baptized will be saved; but he who does not believe will be condemned. And these signs will accompany those who believe: in my name they will cast out demons; they will speak in new tongues; they will pick up serpents, and if they drink any deadly thing, it will not hurt them; they will lay their hands on the sick; and they will recover' (16.15–18).

This is at variance to Jesus' teaching during his life. This command more clearly reflects the aspirations of the early church or perhaps more accurately that of the author. Jesus then ascends into heaven.

Matthew

Matthew (28.1–20) describes Mary Magdalene and another Mary approaching the tomb on Sunday morning when there was a severe earthquake and an angel with the appearance of lightning and 'his raiment as white as snow' appeared. The angel rolled back the stone. The guards present were terrified. The angel reassures the women that Jesus has risen from the dead and is proceeding to Galilee. As they rushed to tell the disciples they met Jesus 'and took hold of his feet and worshipped him'. Jesus tells them not to be afraid but to go to Galilee. Matthew then describes how the guards go to the high priest to report what had happened. The guards are bribed to say that whilst they were asleep the disciples stole Jesus' body, an account that gained some credence amongst the Jews. The eleven disciples return to Galilee. 'And when they saw him they worshipped him but some doubted.' Jesus then says, 'Go therefore and make disciples of all nations, baptizing them in the name of the Father and of the Son and of the Holy Spirit, teaching them to observe all that I have commanded you; and lo, I am with you always, to the close of the age'. There is no mention of his ascension to heaven.

Luke

In Luke (24.1–53), Mary Magdalene and other women go to the tomb with spices but find the stone rolled away but no body. They were perplexed but two men 'in dazzling apparel' explained, 'Remember how he told you, while he was still in Galilee, that the Son of man must be delivered into the hands of sinful men, and be crucified, and on the third day rise'. The women return to recount their experience to 'the eleven and all the rest'. However, 'these words seemed to them an idle tale, and they did not believe them'.

Later that day, two followers of Jesus were walking the seven miles to Emmaus when they were joined by a stranger. One is named Cleopas, the husband of Jesus' aunt called Mary. They were discussing the events of the previous few days. The stranger interpreted the events in the light of scripture that the Messiah had first to suffer and then be glorified. The stranger was invited to stay with them. As they shared a meal, 'He [Jesus] took the bread and blessed, and broke it, and gave it to them. And their eyes were opened and they recognised him; and he vanished out of their sight'. They immediately return to Jerusalem to report to the disciples and others.

As they recount the story, Jesus appears among them. 'They were startled and frightened, and supposed they saw a spirit'.

Jesus says, 'See my hands and feet, that it is I myself; handle me, and see; for a spirit has not flesh and bones as you see that I have.' Jesus then ate some broiled fish. He explains that, 'Everything written about me in the Law of Moses and the prophets and the Psalms must be fulfilled'. He interprets this, 'It is written, that the Christ should suffer and on the third day rise from the dead, and that repentance and forgiveness of sins should be preached in his name to all nations, beginning from Jerusalem'. Jesus instructs them to stay in Jerusalem until they have received the Holy Spirit. However Jesus leads them to Bethany where, after blessing them, he parted from them and was carried up into heaven. The disciples return to Jerusalem 'and were continually in the Temple blessing God'.

John

John (20.1–31) gives the most detailed account of the resurrection. Mary Magdalene goes alone to the tomb, before sunrise on Sunday, to find that the stone had been taken away. She runs to Simon Peter and an anonymous disciple to tell them that 'They have taken the Lord out of the tomb, and we do not know where they have laid him'. Both disciples rush to the tomb and on entering it find 'the linen cloths lying, and the napkin, which had been on his head, not lying with the linen cloths but rolled up in a place by itself'. The disciples make no comment as 'they did not know the scripture that he must rise from the dead'. The disciples leave the scene but Mary remains in tears. She sees two angels 'sitting where the body of Jesus had lain' and tells them that she is crying 'because they have taken away my Lord, and I do not know where they have laid him'. The angels offer no explanation but Mary becomes aware of someone standing behind her. She turns but not recognising the person assumes him to be the gardener. Mary's initial reaction to the empty tomb is repeated, 'Sir, if you have carried him away, tell me where you have laid him, and I will take him away'. It is only when he calls her by her name does she recognise the voice as that of Jesus and calls him 'Teacher'. Jesus responds, 'Do not hold me, for I have not yet ascended to the Father; but go to my brethren and say to them, I am ascending to my Father and your Father, to my God and your God'.

That evening the disciples were frightened, expecting further reprisals from the Jews. They were in a room with the doors shut when Jesus appeared among them. He said, 'Peace be with you.' He showed them his hands and side. He then breathed on them saying, 'Receive the Holy Spirit. If you forgive the sins of any, they are forgiven; if you retain the sins of any, they are retained.' When the disciples described their experience to Thomas, who was not with them at the time, he responded, 'Unless I see in his hands the print of the nails, and place my finger in the mark of the nails, and place my hand in his side, I will not believe.' Eight days later, Jesus again appears to the disciples in a closed house and instructs Thomas to feel his hands and side. Thomas responds, 'My Lord and my God!' Jesus said to him, 'Have you believed because you have seen me? Blessed are those who have not seen and yet believe.'

It is generally believed that John completed his gospel at this point but chapter twenty-one was added as an appendix. Jesus makes another appearance to some of the disciples, not in Jerusalem but in Galilee. Seven of them had been fishing all night on the Sea of Tiberias without any success, when a stranger on the shore instructs them to cast their net on the other side of the boat. The net was so full of fish that they could not haul it in. It was then that they realised that the stranger was Jesus. He had lit a charcoal fire and together they shared a meal of bread and fish. John only indirectly refers to Jesus' ascension.

The emphasis in John's understanding of Jesus is summarised thus, 'I [Jesus] came from the Father and have come into the world; again, I am leaving the world and going to the Father' (16.28).

Comparative Readings and Discussions

Even a superficial reading of the four accounts of Jesus' resurrection reveals significant discrepancies. To commence with themes that are common to all accounts. Early on Sunday morning Mary Magdalene, either alone (John) or accompanied by other women, go to the tomb. There they find the stone in front of the tomb rolled back and the tomb empty. Jesus then

147

makes several different appearances to his close followers but to no one else. Nevertheless, none of his friends recognise him until he reveals his identity. Mary Magdalene thinks he is the gardener; on the road to Emmaus and by the Sea of Tiberias he is a stranger. When he appeared to the disciples in a closed room in Jerusalem they thought that they had seen a ghost and only believed when he showed them his hands and side. Paul (1 Corinthians 15.6) maintain that Jesus 'appeared to more than five hundred brethren', but there is no mention of this in the gospels.

Attempts to reconstruct the events following the discovery of the empty tomb as historical narrative face great difficulties. It is worth enumerating some of the inconsistencies.

- Did Mary Magdalene go to the tomb alone or was she accompanied by one, two or several women?
- Had the stone been rolled back or did an angel do this and in the process terrify the guards?
- When Mary Magdalene arrived at the tomb, were there one, two or no angels present?
- Did the angels say that Jesus had returned to Galilee and this was subsequently forgotten or was it deliberately omitted from two accounts?
- Only in Matthew do the disciples return to Galilee where Jesus appears to them on a mountain but 'some doubted'. Matthew makes no reference to any appearances to the disciples in Jerusalem. Jesus' appearance at the Sea of Tiberias occurs some time later in the appendix to John's gospel.
- In Luke, Jesus tells his disciples to stay in Jerusalem until they receive the Holy Spirit.
- Did Mary Magdalene take hold of Jesus' feet or did Jesus tell her not to touch him? The latter account is given by John who later has Thomas feeling his wounds.
- Accounts of Jesus' ascension to heaven vary. In Mark it happens on that Sunday from Jerusalem. Matthew makes no direct mention but presumably it occurred from the mountain in Galilee. In Luke the ascension occurs from Bethany on that Sunday. However, in

148

writing the Acts of the Apostles he states that Jesus remained with the disciples for forty days, ascending from the Mount of Olivet. John makes no direct reference to the ascension but implies that Jesus returned to his Father from whom he came at the time of his resurrection.

In spite of this there are some themes common to all accounts that deserve further consideration.

The most remarkable feature was that none of his followers expected Jesus to rise from the dead. Following his crucifixion the picture portrayed is of a terrified, confused and demoralised group of disciples. This was in spite of the fact that according to the Synoptic Gospels Jesus had predicted his death and resurrection to the disciples. Mark (8.31) wrote:

And he began to teach them that the Son of man must suffer many things, and be rejected by the elders and the chief priests and the scribes, and be killed, and after three days rise again.

The same message is repeated by Luke (9.22) and Matthew (16.21). In Matthew, Peter responds, 'God forbid, Lord! This shall never happen to you' and the other disciples were greatly distressed (16.22; 17.22). In Mark his message falls on deaf ears, 'But they did not understand the saying and were afraid to ask him' (9.32). It is impossible to assess whether or not Jesus did predict his resurrection or whether the predictions were written after the event. What is clear is that the disciples failed to comprehend Jesus' message. Reasons for their incomprehension is worthy of discussion.

The disciples all came from rural Galilee. Their culture and beliefs were based on their understanding of the Hebrew Scriptures, read on the Sabbath in synagogues with interpretation given in Aramaic. They were not immersed in the world of Greek culture. To understand how they conceived death we have to turn to the Old Testament. As a consequence of eating from the forbidden tree of knowledge God tells them, 'In the sweat of your face you shall eat bread till you return to the ground, for out of it you were taken; you are dust, and to dust you will return.' (Gen. 3.19) Death was accepted as the inevitable end. Thus:

> When David's time to die drew near, he charged Solomon his son, saying, 'I am about to go the way of all the earth. Be strong, and show yourself a man, and keep the charge of the Lord your God' (1 Kings 2.1-3).

Psalm 13 is a plea to God for help in this life:

> How much longer will you forget me, Yahweh? For ever?...
> Give my eyes light, or I shall sleep in death,
> and my enemy will say, 'I have beaten him'...
> Let my heart rejoice in your saving help (Ps. 13.1,3,4 JB).

The Psalmist is praying for help before his unending sleep of death.

Job succinctly summarises traditional belief in Old Testament times 'Man has a short life. He blossoms, and he withers, like flower; fleeting as a shadow, transient'. He draws an analogy with a tree that is cut down but provided its roots have water will sprout to life again.

> But man? He dies and lifeless he remains; man breathes his last, and then where is he? But man, once in his resting place, will never rise again. The heavens will wear away before he wakes, before he rises from his sleep (Job 14.1–2; 10–12 JB).

In Ecclesiastes (3.19–22) we read:

> For the fate of the sons of men and the fate of beasts is the same; as one dies, so dies the other. They all have the same breath, and man has no advantage over the beasts; for all is vanity. All go to one place; all are from the dust, and all turn to dust again... So I saw that there is nothing better than that a man should enjoy his work, for that is his lot.

All the dead, whether good or evil, rich or poor, slave or free go down to Sheol, a bleak subterranean region (Job 3.11–9). There they subsist only as impotent shadows cut off from God and human life. When the Hebrew scriptures was translated into Greek the name Sheol was translated as Hades. This resulted in some Greek mythological connotations and association with the god Hades who ruled over it.

There are some exceptions. Ezekiel (37.1–14) writing about the Jews in exile describes a valley full of bones representing the defeated people of Israel. God breathes life into them and they become covered with flesh and skin and stand up. This symbolised the rebirth of the nation. It resonated two and a half thousand years later in the Negro spiritual 'Dry Bones'.

Judaism was and is an evolving faith. It was natural that they should ask the perennial human question, 'How long shall the wicked exult?' (Ps. 94.3) or 'Why does the way of the wicked prosper? Why do all who are treacherous thrive?' (Jeremiah 12.1). The Pharisees began to wrestle with this problem about 200 BC. During the Maccabaean period Jews were prepared to sacrifice their lives rather than deny their faith. They were the first Jewish martyrs. If God is just, surely these martyrs deserve a better fate than Sheol. The concept of resurrection was a possible solution to the problem. Some Pharisees living in Israel favoured resurrection of the body whereas those in the Gentile world favoured the concept of a soul released from the restraints of the human body. By the second century AD Pharisaic-rabbinic religion encompassed belief in bodily resurrection.

We return to the question as to why the disciples did not understand what Jesus meant by resurrection. To the Sadducees, the aristocratic rulers of the Temple, Sheol was the fate of all men. This would have been the teaching in the synagogues. We do not know what proportion of the Pharisees believed in resurrection. In any event they lived in Jerusalem or the neighbouring cities in Judea. We know from Josephus that there were very few Pharisees in Galilee and these were probably only visiting. The concept of resurrection would not have surfaced in the synagogues of Galilee, hence the disciples' incomprehension.

The other common feature to all accounts is the firm conviction that Jesus, after his death, had appeared perhaps in various guises to his close followers. To them this was a very real experience and motivated their subsequent behaviour. Such experiences were not unique to the disciples. Even people in Western secular cultures record similar experiences today. Perhaps an understanding of the psychology of bereavement may be more valuable than a historian's approach to the subject and the mystery of the resurrection.

Numerous attempts have been made to explain the empty tomb without recourse to supernatural phenomena. That Mary Magdalene and possibly other women who had watched Jesus' internment went to the wrong tomb is improbable. That the disciples removed the body is incredible as they did not expect his resurrection and would not explain their subsequent behaviour. Baigent's *The Jesus Letters* proposed that with the connivance of Pontius Pilate Jesus was taken down alive, nursed back to health and enjoyed fifteen to twenty years in marital bliss with Mary Magdalene in Egypt. The book was based on the 'discovery' of two long Aramaic letters on papyrus that Baigent could not read. The papyri were never seen by scholars in the field and have disappeared (quoted in Vermes, 2009, p.166, 167). The Ahmadiyya sect of Islam interpret the Koran as showing that Jesus did not die on the cross but emigrated to India, ending his life in Kashmir (quoted in Vermes, 2009, p.167). There may be many doubts about the historical Jesus as portrayed in the New Testament but his death on the cross is undisputable.

The internment of Jesus has to be considered in the context of Jewish burial traditions. Josephus wrote:

> The Jews used to take so much care of the burial of men, that they took down those that were condemned and crucified, and buried them before the going down of the sun (Josephus, *Wars,* 4:5:2).

The tradition goes back to Abraham's purchase of a cave for the burial of Sarah (Genesis 23.4–19), to the burial accounts of the patriarchs and kings of Israel. Even the wicked and divinely judged are buried too, such as those in the wilderness who were greedy for meat (Num. 11.33–34). Israel's enemies, slain in battle, are buried (1 Kings 11.15) including the allegorical enemy hosts of Gog (Ezek. 39.11–16).

This practice has its origins in Mosaic Law:

> And if a man has committed a crime punishable by death and he is put to death, and you hang him on a tree, his body shall not remain all night upon the tree, but you shall bury him the same day, for a hanged man is accursed by God; you shall not defile your land which the Lord your God gives you for an inheritance (Deut. 21.22–23).

Joseph of Arimathea was acting in accordance with Jewish tradition when he interred Jesus in a newly hewn cavern in the rock. This was intended as the family grave. This was the privilege of the rich as most people were buried. The body would lie in the tomb for a year until all the flesh had disintegrated. The bones would then be placed in a box made of limestone, or occasionally wood called an ossuary.

As discussed earlier, the conviction, crucifixion and internment of Jesus all took place within six to nine hours. Joseph of Arimathea would have used the tomb impetuously out of respect for Jesus without time for consultation with his family. On hearing of his action, his wife would presume that he had desecrated their family tomb. Another aspect of Mosaic Law may have influenced her. In the event of a man dying in a tent, not only those present but the tent and its contents are regarded as unclean.

> For the unclean they shall take some ashes of the burnt sin offering, and running water shall be added in a vessel; then a clean person shall take hyssop, and dip it in water, and sprinkle it upon the tent, and upon all the furnishings, and upon the persons who were there (Num. 19.17–18).

Would she have thought that placing the corpse of what she probably considered a crucified criminal in the family burial chamber would render it unclean? Or perhaps she simply could not bear the thought of her family being interred in the same chamber as this man. Joseph of Arimathea's wife would have had justifiable reasons for removing Jesus' body as quickly as possible. This would be a very human reaction as to where one should be buried even today. I remember a divorced couple living in France losing a young son. At the father's insistence the son was placed in his family's mausoleum. Sometime later the mother secretly transferred her son's coffin to her family's mausoleum away from past family members with dubious reputations. Some years later she died and gained comfort in the thought that she would be placed to rest next to her son. Whether or not Joseph of Arimathea's wife moved Jesus' body is pure conjecture. What is certain is that subsequently Jesus yet rose in the hearts of his disciples who had loved him and felt that he was near. This is the subject of the next chapter.

X

The Disciples' Response to their Experience of the Resurrection

Our knowledge of this period is dependent on Luke in his sequel to his gospel, the Acts of the Apostles. According to Luke, the disciples did not return to Galilee, as implied in Matthew, but remained in Jerusalem where Jesus appeared to them over a period of forty days and spoke to them of the kingdom of God. Jesus' final words before his ascension were, 'You shall receive power when the Holy Spirit has come upon you; and you shall be my witnesses' (Acts 1.8). Immediately after Jesus' crucifixion, the disciples remained in the room in which they had been staying together with Mary the mother of Jesus and his brothers. By this time Judas had committed suicide and it was decided that he should be replaced. Two men who had accompanied Jesus from his baptism to his ascension were selected. Lots were cast for God to make the appropriate choice. Matthias was appointed.

Jerusalem would have been crowded with pilgrims attending the Feast of Weeks to celebrate the giving of the Torah to Moses. The festival occurred seven weeks after Passover. Using their lunar calendar this equated to fifty days, hence the New Testament's expression 'Pentecost'. On this day they were all in one place. Luke does not make it clear whether all refers to the one hundred and twenty close followers of Jesus (Acts 1:15) or just the twelve disciples, but either way:

> Suddenly a sound came from heaven like the rush of a mighty wind, and it filled all the house where they were

155

sitting. And there appeared to them tongues as of fire, distributed and resting on each one of them. And they were all filled with the Holy Spirit and began to speak in other tongues, as the Spirit gave them utterance (Acts 2.2–4).

In other words, they experienced glossolalia and spoke in other languages although elsewhere 'speaking in tongues' includes unintelligent utterances (1 Corinthians 14). Such behaviour drew the attention of the Diaspora Jews attending the festival. Some were amazed and perplexed whilst others thought that they were drunk.

Peter addresses the crowd pointing out that as it was only nine o'clock in the morning they were not drunk. Their apparent madness was Hebrew Scriptures prophesy being fulfilled. He quotes from Joel (2.28–32):

And in the last days it shall be, God declares, that I will pour out my spirit on all flesh, and your sons and daughters shall prophesy, and your young men shall see visions, and your old men shall dream dreams (Acts 2.17).

When Joel referred to 'all flesh' he was referring exclusively to the Jews and this is how Peter and his audience would have understood it. Peter then describes the disciples' eye-witness accounts of the death, resurrection and ascension of Jesus to the right hand of God. Finally, Peter exhorts his audience to, 'Repent, and be baptized every one of you in the name of Jesus Christ for the forgiveness of your sins; and you shall receive the gift of the Holy Spirit' (Acts 2.38). Luke records that three thousand people were baptized that day.

Those who had been baptized formed a community who sold all their possessions and distributed them to who had need (Acts 2.45). They attended the Temple and shared bread in their homes. Peter and John were confronted by a man, over forty years old, lame from birth begging for alms at the gate to the Temple called Beautiful. Peter responds, 'I have no silver or gold, but I give you what I have; in the name of Jesus Christ of Nazareth, walk' (Acts 3.6). The lame man makes an immediate recovery to the amazement of the people present. Peter explains that it is not his power to heal:

> But by faith in his name [Jesus], has made this man strong whom you see and know, and the faith which is through Jesus has given the man this perfect health in the presence of you all (Acts 3.16).

Peter then tells them to repent.

The Sadducees arrested Peter and John because they were teaching in the Temple and 'proclaiming in Jesus the resurrection from the dead' (Acts 4.2) which was contrary to their belief. In contrast to Matthew and Mark's accounts of the trial of Jesus they were held in prison overnight 'for it was already evening' (Acts 4.3). The Sanhedrin presumably could not lawfully meet at night. Luke says that the Sanhedrin met the following day presided over by the high priest Annas but it must have been Caiaphas his son-in-law who then presided as Annas held the post, 6–15 AD. The inquiry was not directly concerned with resurrection but with the power and authority of the name of Jesus. Peter's ironical opening is to question why he is being examined by a criminal court concerning a good deed of healing (Acts 4.9). He then proceeds to explain how that very court had condemned Jesus to death but God had raised him up. Peter and John were removed from the court whilst they deliberated. They considered the accused as 'bold' in the sense of a servant questioning his master, 'uneducated and common men' or illiterate and amateurish as opposed to educated and professional. However, in the presence of the healed man they had no alternative but to warn them 'not to speak or teach in the name of Jesus'. But Peter and John answered them:

> Whether it is right in the sight of God to listen to you rather than to God, you must judge; for we cannot but speak of what we have seen and heard (Acts 4.18–20).

After further threats, they were released.

Undeterred, the disciples continued to preach in the Temple, cure the sick and cast out unclean spirits attracting people from the neighbouring towns. Again Peter and John are arrested and imprisoned. In the morning officers go to collect them and find the prison doors locked and the sentries still on duty but they have miraculously escaped. They are promptly rearrested as they taught in the Temple. Members of the Sanhedrin wished to kill them but a highly respected Pharisee named Gamaliel intervened. There had been false prophets in the past but their influence had been short-lived. If this is the work of God 'you will not be able to overthrow them' (Acts 5.33–39). Luke quotes Gamaliel as giving examples of two false prophets, Theudas and later a Galilean called Judas. Theudas' uprising occurred much later than the trial in about 48 AD and Judas opposed the census in 6 AD, but his sons, James and Simon led a revolt in the early fifties. Luke's chronology cannot be supported but his argument is valid. After being beaten, Peter and John are released.

The disciples continued to preach and to heal with increasing numbers of people joining their community. They continued to share all their possessions. A dispute broke out between the Aramaic-speaking Jews of Palestine and the Greek-speaking Jews of the Diaspora. The latter felt that they were not getting their fair share of the daily distribution. The disciples believed that it was their role to continue preaching rather than serve at tables. Seven men were chosen to undertake the task of sharing resources. It is noteworthy that they all had Greek names. One of those appointed was Stephen who in addition to his appointed duties 'did great wonders and signs among the people'.

It appears that Stephen started preaching in the synagogues of the Jews of the Diaspora in Jerusalem. Luke's text is a little ambiguous (Acts 6.8–15). However they accuse Stephen of blasphemous attacks against the Law and the Temple and he is brought in front of the Sanhedrin. Stephen's speech is extremely long, comprising fifty-three verses. It is not a defence against the charges on which he was tried rather an exposition of his faith in Jesus. Luke seems to address it to the reader rather than the supposed audience. Stephen gives a panoramic view of God's dealing with Israel from Abraham, through Isaac, Jacob, Joseph,

Moses, Joshua David and Solomon. Stephen argued that the Jews had betrayed Joseph, rejected Moses, turned to idols, broke the Law and sterilised their religion in an almost idolatrous devotion to the man-made Temple. They were continuing their tradition of resisting God's message in their failure to regard Jesus as Messiah. Finally, Stephen directly attacks the contemporary leaders, the Sadducees.

'You stiff necked people, uncircumcised in heart and ears, you always resist the Holy Spirit. As your fathers did, so do you' (Acts 7.51). This was not well received: 'Now when they heard these things they were enraged, and they ground their teeth against him' (Acts 7.54). Stephen was found guilty of blasphemy and 'Then they cast him out of the city and stoned him' (Acts 7.58).

Stephen's speech caused a radical split in the early Christian ranks. It provoked a hostile response from Orthodox Judaism. On the day of Stephen's death 'a great persecution arose against the church in Jerusalem; and they were all scattered throughout the region of Judea and Samaria, except the apostles' (Acts 8.1). The persecution was directed against the Hellenist Jews whilst the apostles, who continued to worship in the Temple, were considered to be part of the Jewish tradition. According to Luke, a prominent figure in the persecution was a Pharisee called Saul. He had looked after the clothes of the witnesses responsible for the stoning of Stephen and had expressed his agreement with the sentence. He continued the persecution and 'laid waste the church and entering house after house, he dragged off men and women and committed them to prison' (Acts 8.3).

Our attention now turns to Saul. That was his Jewish name but soon afterwards he used his Roman name, Paul. He was a man with great energy, courage and vision. Almost single-handedly, he laid the foundations of the Church in Syria, Asia Minor and Europe. Arguably, without the influence of Paul, the followers of Jesus would have remained a small sect within Judaism who would have become increasingly disillusioned as the kingdom of God failed to materialise as a temporal reality and they would have faded away. It is Paul's contribution to Christian belief that we next consider.

XI

Paul's Influence on the Early Church

Paul was born in Tarsus in Cilicia, now Turkey, close to the Eastern extreme of its Mediterranean coastline. Tarsus was a thriving and sophisticated Greek city. It was a key trading centre with a university and an important centre of the Stoic philosophy. It was here that Cleopatra sailed in her gilt barge to meet Mark Anthony in 41BC. Paul's parents were both Jews of the tribe of Benjamin and early church tradition maintained that they came from Galilee. His father must have been an influential person as he was awarded Roman citizenship which Paul inherited. He remained a proud supporter of the Roman Empire throughout his life. We know nothing about his early life but at some stage he went to Jerusalem and studied under the famous Pharisee, Gamaliel and became a Pharisee himself.

Our knowledge of Paul and the early church is derived from Luke's Acts of the Apostles and the letters of Paul. The latter were written in a short period in the fifties thus predating the gospels by about two to four decades. They are the earliest indication of the prevailing thought at the time. Biblical scholars believe that not all the Epistles ascribed to Paul in the New Testament were written by him. Some were written by followers of Paul and it would have been normal practice to ascribe them to their teacher. The letter to the Hebrews is generally thought not to be the work of Paul. Other letters are more controversial but this need not concern us as they all reflect early Christian thought. In the New Testament they are arranged in a rather arbitrary manner rather than in the chronological order in which they were written. There are significant discrepancies between

Paul's letters and Luke's account. Paul describes bitter controversies in the early church. Luke smooths over the issues.

Following Paul's acquiescence in the stoning of Stephen, with the authority of the high priest, he proceeded to Damascus to persecute followers of Jesus in the synagogues there. Paul's motivation, as he recorded later, was because he was 'so extremely zealous for the traditions of my fathers' (Gal. 1.14). As he approached Damascus he had a vision that he describes as a revelation. 'The gospel that was preached by me was not man's gospel [human message]. For I did not receive it from man, nor was I taught it, but it came through a revelation of Jesus Christ.' (Gal. 1.11–12).

Paul saw a bright light; he fell to the ground and heard a voice, 'Saul, Saul, why do you persecute me? And he said, "Who are you Lord?" And he said, "I am Jesus whom you are persecuting; but rise and enter the city, and you will be told what to do"' (Acts 9.4–6).

Paul was literally blinded by the experience and was taken to Damascus. Three days later, a disciple called Ananias is prompted by a vision to visit Paul but was very reluctant to go because of Paul's reputation. He is reassured that Paul is 'a chosen instrument of mine to carry my name before the Gentiles and kings and the sons of Israel'. He visits Paul, restores his sight and baptizes him. This must be the most dramatic conversion in Christian history. There is no rational explanation for Paul's conversion. It was not an intellectual understanding of the life and teaching of Jesus. The reality was that Paul was convinced he had personally experienced the risen Christ and this was to be his dominant message for the rest of his life. Paul describes how Jesus appeared to the disciples, 'to more than five hundred brethren at the same time' and 'last of all, as to one untimely born [unexpected], he appeared also to me' (1 Cor. 15.6–8). It is a central tenet of Christian belief today.

According to Luke, Paul stayed in Damascus for several days, preaching in the synagogues. Some did not trust him and planned to kill him. Paul escaped by being lowered down over the city walls in a basket. He then returned to Jerusalem wishing to join the disciples but they were reluctant to meet him. Barnabas secured reconciliation. Some of the Hellenist Jews whom he had previously persecuted sought to kill him and he fled to Tarsus (Acts 9.19–30). Paul's account of events immediately after Damascus is rather different. He describes how God had revealed his Son to him so that he could preach to the Gentiles:

'I did not confer with flesh and blood, nor did I go up to Jerusalem to those who were apostles before me, but I went away to Arabia; and again I returned to Damascus. Then after three years I went up to Jerusalem to visit Cephas [Peter], and remained with him fifteen days. But I saw none of the other apostles except James the Lord's brother. (In what I am writing to you, before God, I do not lie!) Then I went into the regions of Syria and Cilicia' (Gal. 1.16–21).

From a historical perspective, Paul's account is probably the more accurate. Luke was writing about thirty to forty years later and tries to gloss over differences in the early Church to give an image of harmony. Why did Paul go to Arabia, possibly the Negev desert south of Beersheba? It has been suggested that he went there to contemplate and develop his Christian doctrine. There are plenty of analogies such as Elijah, John the Baptist or various mystics. This is not the Paul of the New Testament, who was a man of action with a sense of urgency about his mission. Paul was not a philosopher and his message was relatively straightforward. To Paul, Jesus' revelation to him was not just a personal experience but a command to preach the good news to the Gentiles. This was urgent as Paul believed that Jesus would return to inaugurate his kingdom soon. Perhaps, having been forced to flee Damascus, Paul felt he should take the good news to Gentiles who were unaware of his earlier activities. This was not an uninhabited region as it is today, Petra was in the vicinity. Yet it appears that his message fell on deaf ears.

Many are surprised that it took Paul three years before he made contact with those who had known Jesus. In his Epistles, there are scant references to Jesus' activities or teaching. To Paul this was of peripheral interest because Jesus became the Son of God by his resurrection and not before:

> From now on, therefore, we regard no one from a human point of view; even though we once regarded Christ from a human point of view, we regard him thus no longer (2 Cor. 5.16).

Paul regarded Jesus' life on earth as irrelevant to his message. When Paul visited Jerusalem some three years after his conversion it appears as though he had a cool reception. He only met Peter (Cephas) and James and they must have felt rather dubious about this new believer but there is no evidence of any direct hostility at this stage. Peter and James reserved their judgment and adopted a policy of wait and see. Paul's itinerary on leaving Jerusalem is shrouded in mystery. It is probable that he visited Antioch. This was the capital of Syria, the third largest city in the world after Rome and Alexandria. It is now the Turkish city of Antakya. At the time it was a flourishing cosmopolitan city with magnificent temples, colonnades, open spaces and swimming pools. It accommodated a significant Jewish community partly due to its relatively easy access from Jerusalem. The fledgling church in Antioch was founded by Hellenistic Jews fleeing after Stephen's death. The early church flourished and the followers became known as Christians for the first time. On hearing of this development, the Jerusalem church sent Barnabas to investigate. To assist in his task, Barnabas went to seek Paul in Tarsus to accompany him. Barnabas and Paul spent a year preaching in Antioch (Acts 11.19–26). We can imply that Paul at this stage had the tacit support of those in Jerusalem. Barnabas then accompanied Paul on his first missionary journey to Cyprus, Syria and Asia Minor. There we have the first account of Paul converting a Gentile, the Roman governor Sergius Paulus to Christianity. The conversion was opposed by the magician Elymas. Paul demonstrated his superior power by rendering him temporally blind (Acts 13.6–12). This must have been a significant conversion for Paul. Whilst most

Jews hated the Romans, Paul had the highest respect for the Roman Empire; after all he was a Roman citizen. He was later to write in detail on the subject (Romans 13.1–7). To quote but briefly:

> Let every person be subject to the governing authorities. For there is no authority except from God, and those that exist have been instituted by God. Therefore he who resists the authorities resists what God has appointed, and those who resist will incur judgement. For the same reason you also pay taxes, for the authorities are ministers of God, attending to this very thing.

The concept of 'the Divine Right of Kings' dates back to the Old Testament but Paul gives it a moral justification that would shape Western civilisation for almost two thousand years. On the other hand he frequently condemns the immoral behaviour of many Roman citizens. Paul's attitude to Roman authority would not have enamoured him to the church in Jerusalem.

The Admission of Gentiles to the Christian Community

When Paul and Barnabas returned to Antioch, representatives of the church in Jerusalem were insisting that circumcision was a prerequisite to salvation. A bitter row ensued. Paul and Barnabas headed a delegation to attempt to resolve the issue in Jerusalem. As they travelled through Phoenicia and Samaria many Gentiles were converted. In Jerusalem they were confronted with the view that, 'It is necessary to circumcise them, and to charge them to keep the Law of Moses' (Acts 15.5). The followers of Jesus in Jerusalem, often referred to as Nazarenes, continued to be faithful to their Jewish faith, worshipping in the Temple and following the Law of Moses. They had the added belief in the imminent arrival of the kingdom of God as expressed in the Old Testament and predicted by Jesus. Jesus' message had been to the Jews and their expectation was that Jesus' triumphal return would inaugurate Jewish supremacy. This would be the fulfilment of God's covenant with Abraham but this was on condition that all males were circumcised:

> Any uncircumcised male who is not circumcised in the flesh of his foreskin shall be cut off from his people; he has broken my covenant (Gen. 17.14).

The ruling also applied to any slaves employed by Jews in their households. Furthermore, how could they abrogate the Torah? As we have seen earlier, unlike the New Testament descriptions, the Law of Moses was to them a liberating experience not an impossible obligation. Throughout the Old Testament they are exhorted to be holy. This meant to be distinctive and separate from the Gentiles. Under these circumstances it is difficult to visualise an amicable agreement.

A precedent had been set for the ensuing debate by Peter's baptism of Cornelius. (Acts 10.1–48) He was a Roman centurion based in Caesarea who together with his family was devout and God fearing. He gave generously to Jewish causes and was highly regarded in Jewish circles. An angel appeared to him in a vision indicating that his alms had been accepted as a sacrifice in the sight of God and instructing him to send for Peter who was staying in Jaffa. Servants were dispatched. At about the same time, Peter also had a vision. A large sheet was lowered to earth containing every sort of animal and bird. A voice told him to kill and eat but three times he refused to eat anything profane or unclean. The sheet was then lifted up to heaven. Cornelius' servants arrive and the following day they travel to Caesarea. Cornelius asks Peter to tell him and his household 'what message God has given you for us'. Peter realises the significance of his vision and responds, 'You know it is forbidden for Jews to mix with people of another race and visit them, but God has made it clear to me that I must not call anyone profane or unclean'. He continues, 'Truly I perceive that God shows no partiality [favourites], but in every nation any one who fears him and does what is right is acceptable to him' (Acts 10.34,35). Peter gives a summary of the life, death and resurrection of Jesus concluding that all who believe in Jesus will have their sins forgiven through his name. At this point the Holy Spirit descended on all the listeners and they began speaking in strange languages and praising God. With the visible endorsement of the Holy Spirit, Peter could not but baptize them all. Probably many Jewish Christians would concede that exceptional people such as Cornelius could be baptized but Peter's view that Jesus had died for all men and that the old covenant was over was a step too far.

The council in Jerusalem, presided over by James, arranged to resolve the issue. Peter's argument was that as God had given the Holy Spirit to Gentiles, He approved of taking the Good News to them. Paul and Barnabas described 'all the signs and wonders that had worked' through the Gentiles. James, in his summary, quotes Amos (9.11–12) 'Israel will be restored'. God promised to rebuild the fallen House of David then the rest of mankind would look for the Lord. It was decided unanimously that Paul and Barnabas accompanied by Judas and Silas would return to Antioch with a letter explaining their decision:

> For it has seemed good to the Holy Spirit and to us to lay upon you no greater burden than these necessary things: that you abstain from what has been sacrificed to idols and from blood and from what is strangled and from unchastity. If you keep yourselves from these, you will do well. Farewell (Acts 15.28–29).

It is strange that the Christians in Jerusalem changed their minds so radically in such a short time and that the decision was unanimous. Subsequent actions by members of the church show that the decision was not endorsed by all and the argument persisted. Many regard this as another example of Luke whitewashing the difficulties experienced by the early Christians. Luke was writing when the Christian community was predominantly Gentile and the conditions for entry were minimal. It would have made sense to Luke to predate the change to the council in Jerusalem.

Paul, writing about four or five years after the council in Jerusalem, in his letter to the Galatians, gives a very different picture. The Gentile Christians were being troubled by Jewish

Christians insisting on circumcision and full adherence to the Torah. Paul records how he and Barnabas took a Greek convert Titus with them to Jerusalem. There they met not a full council but only James, Peter and John. It was conceded that Titus 'was not compelled to be circumcised' (Gal. 2.3). They agreed that Paul had been commissioned to preach the Good News to the uncircumcised just as Peter had been commissioned to preach it to the circumcised. This seemed an amicable agreement.

> James, Peter and John, who were reputed to be pillars, gave to me and Barnabas the right hand of fellowship, that we should go to the Gentiles and they to the circumcised; only they would have us remember the poor, which very thing I was eager to do (Gal. 2.9–10).

Paul subsequently collected money from the Gentile converts as a gift to the Jerusalem church. Paul had clearly won his first battle. The power of faith in the sacrificial death of Jesus and his resurrection superseded observance of the Law as a means to salvation. At the same time he had preserved his link with Judaism by maintaining unity with the Jerusalem Church.

In spite of the agreement in Jerusalem, differences soon emerged. Peter visited the church in Antioch and shared meals with the Gentile Christians. When friends of James, who continued to insist on circumcision, arrived and criticised Peter, he severed all links with the Gentiles. Barnabas followed Peter's change of heart. Paul was furious and challenged Peter, 'If you, though a Jew, live like a Gentile and not like a Jew, how can you compel the Gentiles to live like Jews?' (Gal. 2.14).

To Paul, Peter's action reduced the Gentiles to second-rate Christians. He concludes, 'I do not nullify the grace of God; for if justification [righteousness] were through the law, then Christ died to no purpose' (Gal. 2.21). This was a bitter conflict and Paul is forthright in his criticism. Writing to the Philippians he says, 'Look out for the dogs, look out for the evil workers, look out for those who mutilate the flesh [circumcise]' (Phil. 3.2). Or, 'I wish those who unsettle you would mutilate themselves' (Gal 5.12).

Even Luke is unable to paper over the divisions, 'And there arose a sharp contention, so they separated from each other; Barnabas took Mark with him and sailed away to Cyprus, but Paul chose Silas and departed for Syria and Celicia' (Acts 15.39–41). Paul and Barnabas, companions for over twelve years, now parted company in disagreement over circumcision and the Law. Without Paul's determination and tenacity it is doubtful whether the early Christian community would have survived.

Paul continued on his second missionary journey eventually arriving in Thessalonica. Here he gained many converts but some Jews opposed him and accused him of 'acting against the decrees of Caesar, saying that there is another king, Jesus' (Acts 17.7). The civil authorities attempted to arrest Paul but he fled. According to Luke, he had only been there for three weeks (Acts 17.2). Paul was concerned that they had not fully appreciated his message, hence his letters to the Thessalonians. Their pressing concern was that some of them had died before Jesus returns. Paul reassures them that they will be included in the resurrection of the just, although, he thought that he would survive until the Parousia or second coming of Jesus: 'We who are alive, who are left until the coming of the Lord, shall not precede those who have fallen asleep'. Paul uses markedly apocalyptic language. The Lord:

> ...will descend from heaven with a cry of command, with the archangel's call, and the sound of the trumpet of God. And the dead in Christ will rise first; then we who are alive, who are left, shall be caught up together with them in the clouds to meet the Lord in the air; and so we shall always be with the Lord (1 Thess. 4.15–17).

In his second letter to the Thessalonians Paul describes:

> When the Lord Jesus is revealed from heaven with his mighty angels in flaming fire, inflicting vengeance upon those who do not know God and upon those who do not obey the gospel of our Lord Jesus. They shall suffer the punishment of eternal destruction and exclusion from the

presence of the Lord and the glory of his might'. Paul prays that, 'Our God may make you worthy of his call' (2 Thess. 1.7–11).

Writing to the Corinthians about four years later the apocalyptic descriptions are more subdued. He reassures them that:

> We shall not all sleep, but we shall all be changed, in a moment, in the twinkling of an eye, at the last trumpet. For this perishable nature must put on the imperishable, and this mortal nature put on immortality (1 Cor. 15.51–53).

Earlier he explains, 'It is sown as physical body, it will be raised a spiritual body. If there is a physical body, there is also a spiritual body' (1 Cor. 15.44). Here Paul is distancing himself further from traditional Judaism by the concept of a 'spiritual body'. Paul summarises his faith, quoting from Hosea:

> Death is swallowed up in victory. O death, where is thy victory? O death, where is thy sting? The sting of death is sin, and the power of sin is the law. But thanks be to God, who gives us the victory through our Lord Jesus Christ (1 Cor. 15.54–56).

Again, Paul is rejecting the constraints of the Torah.

In the letter to the Romans, Paul changes his emphasis on the resurrection of the dead to the here and now. Jesus' second coming will be the day of judgment but in the meantime baptism represents sharing in Jesus' death and then having the experience to 'walk in the newness of life' (Rom. 6.3).

The letters to the Ephesians and Colossians reflect Paul's cosmic vision where through Jesus the whole universe is reconciled to God: 'According to his [God's] purpose which he set forth in Christ, as a plan for the fullness of time, to unite all things in him, things in heaven and things on earth' (Eph. 1.9–10).

For in him all the fullness of God was pleased to dwell, and through him to reconcile to himself all things, whether on earth or in heaven, making peace by the blood of his cross (Col. 1.19–20).

This theme was developed more fully in John's gospel.
In 56AD Paul made his last visit to Jerusalem. There he faced considerable hostility for baptizing Gentiles who were not circumcised and broke the dietary laws. The controversy had not been resolved. Paul addressed the Sanhedrin but a violent confrontation ensued between the Sadducees and the Pharisees. Fearing for Paul's life – he was a Roman citizen – a tribune took him to the Antonia fortress. Paul was then transferred to the Roman fortress in Caesarea where he was held for two years before being taken to Rome. Luke's account finishes:

> And he lived there two whole years at his own expense, and welcomed all who came to him, preaching the kingdom of God and teaching about the Lord Jesus Christ quite openly and unhindered (Acts 28.30).

In June 64AD the great fire of Rome broke out and Nero blamed the Christians for the destruction. Maybe Nero initiated the fire with the intention of rebuilding the city (quoted in Boardman et al.,1986, p.555). Nevertheless, Nero used the Christians as scapegoats, killing many by crucifixion or by exposure to wild animals in the arena. We do not know when Paul died but it is conceivable that it was a consequence of this period of persecution. Evidence that both Paul and Peter died as martyrs is found in a letter written by Pope Clement in the mid-nineties. Eusebius later wrote:

> It is recorded that in Nero's reign, Paul was beheaded in Rome itself, and that Peter was likewise crucified and the record is confirmed by the fact that the cemeteries there are still called by the names Peter and Paul (quoted. in Stourton 2004 p213).

This may seem dubious evidence, but the church tradition behind it is very strong. Paul's greatest legacy was to admit Gentiles to the Christian fold. Other aspects of his teaching have had a significant effect on Christian thought. These include suffering, his attitude towards women and his understanding of atonement.

Paul's Suffering

Paul showed great fortitude as he faced considerable hardships on his missionary journeys. There were the inevitable dangers of travel at that time but he also faced persecution by the Jews and also by some of his fellow believers. In his second letter to the Corinthians he expresses concern that some followers of Jesus from Jerusalem had been giving a different version of the Gospel from his. The withering sarcasm in chapter eleven shows how deeply he had been hurt by their criticism of him and their depiction of him as a fool:

But whatever any one dares to boast of – I am talking as a fool – I also dare to boast of that. Are they Hebrews? So am I. Are they Israelites? So am I. Are they descendents of Abraham? So am I. Are they servants of Christ? I am a better one – I am talking like a madman – far greater labours, far more imprisonments, with countless beatings, and often near death. Five times I have received at the hands of the Jews the forty lashes less one. Three times I have been beaten with rods; once I was stoned. Three times I have been shipwrecked; a night and a day I have been adrift at sea; on frequent journeys, in danger from rivers, danger from robbers, danger from my own people, danger from Gentiles, danger in the city, danger in the wilderness, danger at sea, danger from false brethren; in toil and hardship, through many a sleepless night, in hunger and thirst, often without food, in cold and exposure. And, apart from other things, there is the daily pressure upon me of my anxiety for all the churches (2 Cor. 11.21–28).

To Paul, life is a struggle and the greater the hardships encountered the prouder one could be:

Do you not know that in a race all the runners compete, but only one receives the prize? So run that you may obtain it. Every athlete exercises self-control in all things. They do it to receive a perishable wreath, but we are imperishable. Well, I do not run aimlessly, I do not box as one beating the air; but I pommel my body and subdue it, lest after preaching to others I myself should be disqualified (1 Cor. 9.24–27).

The analogy to an athlete is apposite. To the Romans, physical prowess and beauty were especially esteemed and rewarded but Paul regarded this as pointless. Similarly, he shows no regard for the achievements of Greek and Roman culture such as its great cities with fine architecture, open spaces and the potential of a comfortable and enjoyable life in well-designed villas. This was not a life he would have desired. As we have seen earlier he admired Roman administration but he detested the lifestyle of its citizens:

They were filled with all manner of wickedness, evil, covetousness, malice. Full of envy, murder, strife, deceit, malignity, they are gossips, slanderers, haters of God, insolent, haughty, boastful, inventors of evil, disobedient to parents, foolish, faithless, heartless, ruthless. Though they know God's decree that those who do such things deserve to die, they not only do them but approve those who practise them (Romans 1.29–32).

Paul was an ascetic and accepted the hardships he endured. Matthew reiterates this belief when he describes how Jesus sent his disciples on a mission, charging them to:

Go nowhere among the Gentiles, and enter no town of the Samaritans, but go rather to the lost sheep of the house of Israel. And preach as you go, saying, 'The kingdom of heaven is at hand.' Heal the sick, raise the dead, cleanse lepers, cast out demons (Matthew 10.5–8).

A few verses later (17–18) Matthew adds a warning:

Beware of men; for they will deliver you up to councils, and flog you in their synagogues, and you will be dragged before governors and kings for my sake, to bear testimony before them and the Gentiles.

The reality was that the disciples suffered no such hardship during Jesus' life and he had forbidden them to go to the Gentiles. Here Matthew is describing a situation that existed when he wrote his gospel and falsely implied that Jesus had predicted this. The picture portrayed of Jesus in the gospels is not that of an ascetic. It is true that he faced hardships, 'Foxes have holes, and birds of the air have nests; but the Son of man has nowhere to lay his head', (Luke 9.58) but Jesus does not eschew the pleasures of life when they are presented to him:

For John came neither eating nor drinking, and they say, 'He has a demon'. The Son of man came eating and drinking, and they say, 'Behold a glutton and a drunkard, a friend of tax collectors and sinners!' (Matthew 11.18–19; Luke 7.33–34).

The ascetic John the Baptist is contrasted with the more relaxed and sociable Jesus, the table companion of publicans and sinners.

For Paul, following Jesus inevitably meant suffering:

We are afflicted in every way, but not crushed; perplexed, but not driven to despair; persecuted, but not forsaken; struck down but not destroyed; always carrying in the body the death of Jesus, so that the life of Jesus may also be manifested in our bodies (2 Cor. 4.8–10).

Paul never sought to suffer for the sake of suffering but rather it was the inevitable consequence of his witness. Subsequent generations have misinterpreted Paul. This was most dramatically demonstrated by the early martyrs. From the days of Herod the Great, the Romans had allowed the Jews freedom to pursue their religious practices. Once Christianity ceased to be part of Judaism, it no longer enjoyed the Jew's religious freedom in the empire. They became a target for persecution when Christians refused to sacrifice to the emperor. Martyrdom quickly became the way of following Christ more perfectly. Well documented is the death of St. Ignatius, Bishop of Antioch and a great admirer of Paul. In the year 107AD, St. Ignatius was taken from Antioch to Rome to face martyrdom. The church in Rome sought his acquittal but he begged them not to do so:

I must implore you to do me no such untimely kindness; pray leave me to be a meal for the beasts, for it is they who can provide my way to God. I am His wheat, ground fine by the lion's teeth to be made purest bread for Christ... When there is no trace of my body left for the world to see, then I shall truly be Jesus Christ's disciple (Armstrong, 1983, p.171).

Ignatius writes that he will coax the lions to be as savage as possible. It is universally accepted that, 'Greater love has no man than this, that a man lay down his life for his friends' (John 15.13). However, Ignatius' fervour for a most cruel death to secure his own salvation can either reflect a pathological state of mind or a degree of dedication deserving of his elevation to sainthood. The second century church father, Tertullian wrote that, 'The blood of martyrs is the seed of Christians' (Quoted in Armstrong, 1983, p.171). Later, within the monastic movement, we see the belief that to experience pain and hardship were enhancing aspects of a spiritual life. Monks would flagellate themselves, immerse themselves all night in ice-cold water, starve and wear hair shirts.

Perhaps of greater significance was Paul's letter to the Corinthians:

174

Everyone should remain in the state in which he was called. Were you a slave when you were called? Never mind. But if you can gain your freedom, avail yourself of the opportunity. For he who was called in the Lord as a slave is a freedman in the Lord. Likewise he who was free when called is a slave of Christ (1 Cor. 7.20–22).

This is understandable in the context of his expectation of the imminent return of Jesus. Unfortunately the Church, over the centuries, has too often accepted the status quo and shown a reluctance to introduce reform in unjust societies. Clearly this is a generalisation and there are significant exceptions but usually by small groups of individuals. The ethos continued to the nineteenth century is exemplified by the popular hymn written in 1848 by Mrs Cecil F. Alexander which commences, 'All things bright and beautiful'. The third verse, which no longer appears in contemporary hymn books, read:

The rich man in his castle,
The poor man at his gate,
God made them high and lowly,
And ordered their estate.

Edward Gibbon in his book *The Decline and Fall of the Roman Empire* attributed the decline in part to the conversion of the Emperor Constantine to Christianity. He wrote, 'the clergy successfully preached the doctrines of patience and pusillanimity; the active virtues of society were discouraged; and the last remains of military spirit were buried in the cloister' (Gibbon, 1960, p.525).

Attitudes to Women and Marriage

From Paul's first letter to the Corinthians it would appear that the church there consisted of an undisciplined congregation. Paul condemns those who partake in incest, frequent prostitutes, eat idolatrous meals, sue one another in pagan courts, and fail to share the Eucharist meal fairly and in the process get drunk.

There were internal factions. Among the dissenting groups were the women expressing their freedom by speaking out in the church and not wearing a veil:

> For if a woman will not veil herself, then she should cut off her hair; but if it is disgraceful for a woman to be shorn or shaven, let her wear a veil. For a man ought not to cover his head, since he is in the image and glory of God; but woman is the glory of man. For man was not made from woman, but woman from man. Neither was man created for woman, but woman for man (1 Cor. 11.6–8).

Paul's insistence on the inferior role of women is reflected in the following passage:

> In all the churches of the saints, the women should keep silence in the churches. For they are not permitted to speak, but should be subordinate, even as the law says. If there is anything they desire to know, let them ask their husbands at home. For it is shameful for a woman to speak in church (1 Cor. 14.33–35).

Perhaps the freedom of expression shown by the women of Corinth was a complete culture shock to Paul hence his vitriolic attack on them. Paul had been brought up in the male-dominated culture of Judaism. Even today the ultra-orthodox Jews or Haredim believe that modesty forbids women to sit at the front of the bus with men and they are segregated to the rear of the bus. On the other hand, Paul's relationship with individual women was more amiable. The first person to be baptzied in Europe was Lydia in Philippi. She was a Gentile and had a successful business in the luxury fashion trade selling purple cloth dyed by extracts from murex shellfish. Paul was happy to accept her hospitality (Acts 16.11–40). Paul asks the Romans to look after Phoebe, a deaconess of the church at Cenchreae and to 'help her in whatever way she may require from you, for she has been a helper of many and of myself as well' (Rom.16.1–2). More importantly, the church in Corinth had two influential

176

members, Aquila and Priscilla. Both were Jewish Christians and had been expelled from Rome by the Emperor Claudius in the year 49AD and ended up in Corinth. Paul stayed with them in Corinth for about eighteen months. They were tent makers, Paul's initial trade (Acts 18.1–3). When Paul decided to proceed to Ephesus, Aquila and Priscilla preceded him as an advanced party. Present in Ephesus was an Alexandrian Jew whose preaching concerning baptism was contrary to their beliefs so, 'They took him and expounded to him the way of God more accurately' (Acts 18.26). They were clearly influential figures in the early church and are mentioned seven times in the New Testament. Contrary to convention, on five occasions Priscilla is mentioned before her husband. Clearly she was not regarded as a second-class citizen. Paul in his letter to the Romans writes:

> Greet Prisca [her Roman name] and Aquila, my fellow workers in Jesus Christ, who risked their necks for my life, to whom not only I but also all the churches of the Gentiles give thanks; greet also the church in their house (Rom. 16.3–5).

Finally, Paul contradicts himself when he writes, 'There is neither Jew or Greek, there is neither slave or free, there is neither male or female; for you are all one in Christ Jesus' (Gal. 3.28).

One has to wonder whether Paul regretted his harsh words to the women in Corinth as in his second letter he writes:

> But I call God to witness against me – it was to spare you that I refrained from coming to Corinth… For I made up my mind not to make you another painful visit (2 Cor. 1.23; 2.1).

However we interpret Paul's attitude to women, his few verses to the women of Corinth continues to profoundly influence the role of women in the church.

For Paul the ideal was to remain celibate, but he accepted that marriage was permissible for those unable to constrain their sexual urges as the lesser evil of temptation to immorality.

Marriage was not an expression of love but the legalisation of sexual appetite.

> To the unmarried and the widows I say that it is well for them to remain single as I do. But if they cannot exercise self-control, they should marry. For it is better to marry than be aflame with passion (1 Cor. 7.8–9).

For those who were already married they should fulfil their conjugal rights and not seek divorce.

> To the married I give charge, not I but the Lord, that her wife should not separate from her husband (but if she does, let her remain single or else be reconciled to her husband) – and that the husband should not divorce his wife (1 Cor. 7.10–11).

However Christians have interpreted Paul's beliefs it is pertinent to point out that these were formulated in the expectation that the second coming of Christ was imminent. This was a temporary state of affairs and all one's efforts should be directed to await his arrival. Paul's teaching became the blueprint for the church's attitude to sexuality with unforeseen consequences that sadly reverberate today with so many unfulfilled or even destroyed lives.

Jesus as a Ransom for many

Central to Christian belief is the concept that, 'The Son of man also came not to be served but to serve, and to give his life as a ransom for many' (Mark 10.45).

In Hebrew the words 'ransom', 'redeem', 'redeemer' and 'redemption' all have the same linguistic root. In the Old Testament this is not a philosophical concept but a concrete and practical transaction. At its simplest, one can pawn an object and then redeem it by paying the appropriate ransom. Similarly it could be the price paid for freeing or acquiring a slave. There are innumerable examples but three will suffice to illustrate the concept. God purchases the release of the Jews in Babylon by paying a ransom to Cyrus, 'I give Egypt as your ransom, Ethiopia and Seba in exchange for you' (Isaiah 43.3).

The book of Ruth was described by Goethe as the loveliest little epic and idyllic whole that tradition has given us. At its heart is a practical example of redemption. At a time of famine, Naomi, her husband and two sons leave Bethlehem to seek better times in Moab. One of the sons marries a Moabite woman, Ruth. Naomi's husband and both sons die. Naomi and Ruth return to Bethlehem destitute. Naomi's husband had owned land in the region. Since there was no heir to inherit the land, levirate custom required a close relative (usually a brother-in-law) to marry the widow of the deceased in order to continue the family line (Deut. 25.5–10). Furthermore, the law of Leviticus (25.25–55) required a kinsman to purchase land back into the family. In Palestine land had to stay in the family. Boaz, a close relative of Naomi's husband but not the closest, in an act of great generosity redeems the land in the presence of witnesses and marries Ruth. He becomes Ruth and Naomi's 'kinsman redeemer'. Incidentally, Boaz and Ruth have a son, Obed, whose grandson is David.

A third example is well known as it appears as an aria in Handel's oratorio, *The Messiah*. It begins, 'I know that my Redeemer liveth' and has inspired generations. Handel is quoting Job (19.25) which is an attempt to address the question as to why we must face loss and pain, frustration and despair. As a sub-theme there is the issue as to why the righteous often suffer and the wicked prosper. The book of Job describes him as an extremely righteous man who had become very prosperous. The 'sons of God' (celestial beings) and 'Satan' (literally the 'adversary') present themselves to God, and God asks Satan his opinion of Job. Satan answers that Job is only pious because God has favoured him with prosperity but were this not the case Job would surely curse God. God gives Satan permission to test Job's righteousness (Job 1.6–12). All of Job's possessions are destroyed: the five hundred yolk of oxen, five hundred donkeys, seven hundred sheep and three thousand camels. Finally his house collapses killing his seven sons and three daughters. In spite of this Job does not curse God but shaves his head and tears his clothes saying, 'Naked I came out of my mother's womb, and naked I shall return: Lord has given, and the Lord has taken away; blessed be the name of the Lord' (Job 1.20–21).

Satan then asks God permission to afflict him personally and God consents provided Job does not die. Satan smites him with dreadful boils, and Job, seated in ashes, scrapes his skin with broken pottery. Job's reputation has been completely destroyed and his despair is reflected in the following verse:

> My brothers stand aloof from me,
> And my relations take care to avoid me.
> My kindred and my friends have all gone away,
> And the guests in my house have forgotten me.
> The serving maids look on me as a foreigner,
> A stranger never seen before.
> My servant does not answer when I call him,
> I am reduced to entreating him.
> To my wife my breath is unbearable,
> For my own brothers I am a thing corrupt (Job 19.13–17 JB).

It is in this context that Job asserts that he knows that his Redeemer lives, 'For I know that my Redeemer lives, and at last he will stand upon the earth' (Job 19:25). Job's redeemer or advocate is a human being who will speak up for him, hopefully before he dies, and clear his reputation with his peers. This is the down to earth practical understanding of redeemer in Old Testament times. The words 'avenger' and 'take his stand' are legal terms to resolve such issues in a court of law. Job had no expectation of a Messiah but Handel must be credited with creating such an evocative aria reflecting salvation as eternal life.

When God is described as redeemer, he acts on behalf of Israel as a worthy kinsman would do for the honour of his kin and the concept of ransom is retained. Speaking of the Israelites' escape from Egypt God says, 'You were sold for nothing, and you shall be redeemed without money' (Isaiah 52.3).

Having redeemed the Israelites he will continue to protect them.

When you pass through the waters I will be with you; and through the rivers, they shall not overwhelm you; when you walk through fire you shall not be burned, and the flame shall not consume you (Isaiah 43.1–2).

As their redeemer God promises them blessings, 'You shall suck the milk of nations, you shall suck the breast of kings; and you shall know that I, the Lord, am your Savior' (Isaiah 60.16).

To give just one other example, 'Fear not, you worm Jacob, you men of Israel! I will help you says the Lord; your redeemer is the Holy One of Israel' (Isaiah 41.14).

In summary, the Old Testament is suffused with the concept of God's redemption of the Israelites and their consequent history. Redemption is for the nation as a whole rather than directed towards individuals. God's activity is seen as primarily a relief from material threats and hardships.

Paul, a Pharisee, had such a profound understanding of the Old Testament that he could boast, 'I advanced in Judaism beyond many of my own age among my people' (Galatians 1.14). Paul's theology is dependent on quotations and allusions to the Old Testament. This is most evident in his letter to the Romans. Thus chapter four is devoted to a reinterpretation of the story of Abraham and chapters nine, ten and eleven are full of quotations from the Old Testament concerning the place of Palestine after the death and resurrection of Jesus. This is the culmination of Palestine's history, the fulfilment of the Law and the Prophets. To Paul Christianity was a continuation of the religion of Israel and was only explicable on those terms. He encouraged Gentile Christians to use the Old Testament, 'For whatever was written in former days was written for our instruction' (Rom. 15.4).

Paul, the great visionary, sees in Jesus' death the accomplishment and synthesis between two great themes of the Old Testament, Temple sacrifice and God's acts of redemption.

Paul's understanding of the death of Jesus is reiterated in all the Epistles, that Jesus gave his life as a ransom for mankind's sins. A few examples will suffice: 'Our Lord Jesus Christ gave himself for our sins to deliver us from the present evil age' (Gal. 1.4).

'In him we have redemption through his blood, the forgiveness of our trespasses, according to the riches of his grace' (Eph. 1.7).

'But God shows his love for us in that while we were yet sinners Christ died for us. Since, therefore, we are now justified by his blood, much more shall we be saved by him from the wrath of God' (Rom. 5.8–9).

> God sent forth his Son, born of a woman, born under the law, to redeem those who were under the law, so that we may receive adoption as sons. So through God you are no longer a slave but a son, and if a son then an heir (Gal. 4.5–7).

Similarly, the author of the letter to the Hebrews makes the transition from Temple practice clear:

> For if the sprinkling of defiled persons with the blood of goats and bulls and with the ashes of a heifer sanctifies for the purification of the flesh, how much more shall the blood of Christ, who through the eternal Spirit offered himself without blemish to God, purify your conscience from dead works to serve the living God (Heb. 9.13–14).

While 'You know that you were ransomed from the futile ways inherited from your fathers, not with perishable things such as silver and gold, but with the precious blood of Christ, like that of a lamb without blemish or spot' (1 Peter 1.18).

Matthew copies a quotation from Mark's Gospel, 'Even as the Son of man came not to be served but to serve, and to give his life as a ransom for many' (Matthew 20.28).

By the time Matthew and Mark were writing their gospels this was a central tenet of Christian belief and they would have had difficulty in imagining that Jesus would not have expressed such a view. This theme is not developed in the Synoptic Gospels nor is it reflected in the teachings of Jesus. Many theologians have questioned whether this was an authentic saying of Jesus.

In a world where sacrifice was part of the ritual of daily life, Paul's explanation of Jesus' sacrifice was met with incredulity from some. Paul responds:

For Jews demand signs and Greeks seek wisdom, but we preach Christ crucified, a stumbling block to Jews and folly to Gentiles, but to those who are called, both Jews and Greeks, Christ the power of God and the wisdom of God. For the foolishness of God is wiser than men, and the weakness of God is stronger than men (1 Cor. 1.22–25).

Paul's faith transcends logic. Since then theologians have argued about Paul's metaphorical use of the concept of Jesus' death being a ransom for many. In the Old Testament, payment of a ransom was a practical transaction such as the payment of money to release a slave. Paul continues the metaphor when he writes, 'You were bought with a price' (1 Cor. 7.23). This raises the insoluble problem as to whom the price was paid. If the price was paid to Satan then this creates a hornets' nest of intractable theological problems. If this were the price God demanded, in the sense of God's wrath being appeased by the sacrifice of his son, then this generates more questions about the Christian's understanding of God. The doctrine of atonement remains a mystery. Nevertheless, to many Christians it is an article of faith that generates profound loyalty and dedication.

To Paul, salvation, rebirth and resurrection depended on faith in Jesus' redeeming act of sacrifice and not on following God's law as revealed in the Torah. Paul tells Cephas (Peter) to his face that, 'We ourselves, who are Jews by birth and not Gentile sinners, yet who know that a man is not justified [reckoned righteous] by works of the law but through faith in Jesus Christ' (Gal. 2.15–16). This would later be a key tenet in the Protestant Reformation.

After Paul's conversion, his first contact with Jesus' disciples was with Peter and James. James was the brother of Jesus and leader of the Christian Jews. It is generally accepted that the letter of James was not written by James but ascribed to him by one of his followers early in the first century, not an uncommon practice. Apparently he was very skilled in the use of the Greek language. What is remarkable about the letter of James, unlike Paul's letters, is that there is no reference to the Gentiles or conditions under which they could be admitted to the Christian community. Faith if it is genuine must be demonstrated by good works. To quote:

> What does it profit, my brethren, if a man says he has faith but has not works? If a brother or a sister is ill-clad and in lack of daily food, and one of you says to them, 'Go in peace, be warmed and filled,' without giving them the things needed for the body, what does it profit? So faith by itself, if it has no works, is dead (James 2.14–17).

Whilst there is a difference between James and Paul on the primacy of faith, the real difference is James' failure to mention the Gentiles, Jesus' resurrection or the concept of atonement. Were these beliefs new to those who had known Jesus during his life on earth? Was the experience of the risen Jesus the catalyst for reforming their beliefs? Were James' followers at the time unfamiliar with the emerging theology? Was Paul's vision of a new understanding of Jesus' significance valid? Paul knew nothing of Jesus' earthly life or teaching. It was John who some seventy years after the death of Jesus formulated an understanding of Christology or God incarnate in Jesus.

In an attempt to answer some of the questions raised in this chapter we need to re-examine the concept of God incarnate.

XII

The Concept of God Incarnate

Orthodox Christian belief is that Jesus was God the Son incarnate, the Second Person of the Trinity living a human life. To explore this concept it is necessary to review the various titles attributed to Jesus in the New Testament. These include 'Son of Man', 'Messiah', 'Christ', 'Son of God' and John's concept of the 'Word made flesh'.

Son of Man

This expression appears sixty-five times in the Synoptic Gospels, eleven times in John, never in Paul and only once in Acts. Christians usually interpret the expression as Jesus emphasising his true humanity; he uniquely was at once God and Man. Some theologians have given a Messianic meaning to the Son of Man based on a dream recorded in Daniel chapter seven. Four terrifying, mystical beasts arose from the sea representing four nations hostile to the Jews. The first three beasts are rendered powerless. The fourth beast develops an additional little horn with eyes and a mouth and sits on a throne of fiery flames. This represented Antiochus IV Epiphanes (175–163BC) of the Seleucid (Syrian) empire who had taken control of Palestine from the Egyptians. He had enforced Greek culture on the Jews including a ban on the observance of the Sabbath. Daniel refers to him as 'the Ancient of Days'. The relevant section reads:

I saw in the night visions, and behold, with the clouds of heaven there came one like the son of man, and he came to the Ancient of Days and was presented before him. And to him was given dominion and glory and kingdom, that all peoples, nations and languages should serve him; his dominion is an everlasting dominion, which shall not pass away, and his kingdom one that shall not be destroyed (Daniel 7.14).

In other words, the son of man defeated the evil fourth beast referred to as the 'Ancient of Days'. The belief that the expression 'like the son of man' represented a messianic figure and that Jesus adopted this name with no explanation is not credible. Daniel, as he explains his dream (Daniel 7.27), makes it clear that 'like the son of man' does not refer to an individual but rather to 'the people of the saints of the Most High' and 'all dominions shall serve and obey them'. This is usually taken to mean that the pious of Israel will have an eschatological triumph.

The 'Son of Man' is the English translation of the Aramaic *bar enasha* or *bar nasha* used to signify oneself. There is no equivalent translation in Greek or English. That Jesus uses the expression to apply to himself is clear when he addresses a paralysed man, 'But that you may know that *the son of Man* has authority on earth to forgive sins... I say to you, Rise' (Mark 2.10).

The expression is never used by others in the Synoptic Gospels but always placed on the lips of Jesus. It is also evident that at no point did Jesus explain any special meaning to the expression nor did anyone question it. It was common parlance in Aramaic. Geza Vermes provides the most coherent explanation. It was a circumlocutional reference to the self-reflecting modesty or humility. The closest we can get to the meaning in English would be the Victorian use of the expression 'yours truly'. For example, 'Who is the author of this splendid article?' or 'Who broke the vase?' may produce the modest or bashful reply, 'Yours truly' rather than a direct, 'I did'. It was in this sense that Jesus used the expression with no theological implications (Vermes, 2000, p.39).

Messiah/Christ

'Messiah' originates from the Hebrew word *mashiach* meaning 'anointed'. It was customary practice to anoint high priests (Exodus 29.7) and kings with oil signifying that they had been chosen by God for their offices. Both Saul and David were anointed and the word became synonymous with 'the King of Israel'. The Hebrew word was taken into Greek as *messias* hence the English 'Messiah'. At the same time they used the Greek word for anointed, *Christos* hence 'Christ'. The origin of the title Christ became blurred in the early Gentile church perhaps because it was pronounced the same as *chrēstos* meaning 'good' or 'kind'. In any event they would not have been interested in a 'Christ' who would restore the kingdom of Israel and vanquish its enemies as believed by the Jews.

The messianic expectation was discussed in chapter seven of the present work. To recapitulate, the expectation is summarised by Zechariah in his blessing of his son, John the Baptist whom he predicts that he will go before the Lord to prepare the way for him. Although presented as a prediction, it must have been composed after the event:

Blessed be the Lord God of Israel,
For he has visited and redeemed his people,
And has raised up a horn of salvation for us
In the house of his servant David,
As he spoke by the mouth of his holy prophets from of old,
That we should be saved from our enemies,
And from the hand of all who hate us (Luke 1.68–73).

The Synoptic Gospels contain few references to the Messiah prior to Jesus' final entry into Jerusalem with the exception of the birth narratives. Jesus even questions the belief that the Messiah could be a descendant of David when he quotes Psalm 110, believed to have been written by David. And as Jesus taught in the Temple, he said:

'How can the scribes say that the Christ is the son of David? David himself, inspired by the Holy Spirit, declared, "The Lord said to my Lord, sit at my right hand, till I put thy enemies under thy feet". David himself calls him Lord; so how is he his son?' (Mark 12.35–37; Matthew 22.41–46; Luke 20.41–44).

This is a rhetorical question with no easy answers.

Jesus' triumphal entry into Jerusalem indicated that a significant number of Jews believed that the kingdom of God was imminent and that Jesus would take the royal throne of David and lead the Jews and vanquish the Romans. But Jesus' teaching was totally apolitical and he would never have contemplated such a role: 'Render to Caesar the things that are Caesar's, and to God the things that are God's' (Mark 12.17).

Jesus' trial was considered in chapter eight of the present work. To recapitulate, Jesus is asked directly by the high priest, 'Are you the Messiah, the son of God?'

In Matthew, Jesus' response is 'It is as you say', neither a denial nor an affirmation. In Luke, Jesus first refuses to answer, 'If I tell you, you will not believe me'. Forced to respond he says, 'It is you who say I am'. Only Mark gives a positive response, 'I am'. Later, when questioned by Pilate as to whether he was king of the Jews he responds, 'You have said so' (Matthew 27.11; Mark 15.2; Luke 23.3). According to Luke, Pilate interprets his answer as negative and says, 'I find no crime in this man.'

Pertinent to the issue is Peter's confession of faith. Jesus '...asked his disciples, "Who do men say that I am?" And they told him, "John the Baptist, and others say Elijah; and others one of the prophets."

And he asked them, "But who do you say that I am?" Peter answered him, "You are the Christ." And he charged them to tell no one about him' (Mark 8.27–30).

Jesus neither confirms nor denies the title. Matthew elaborates the account, possibly to give credence to early Christian belief, with Jesus' response, 'Blessed are you, Simon Bar-Jona! For flesh and blood has not revealed this to you, but my Father who is in heaven' (Matt. 16.15–20). If Jesus had said this, it is difficult to explain why Mark and Luke omit it. A few verses later, Jesus condemns Peter for not being on the side of God and calls him Satan (16.23). Neither Mark nor Luke mentions this episode and its authenticity is open to question. Included in this exchange is the promise, 'You are Peter, and on this rock I will build my church' (16.18). Surely this is a late addition as nowhere else in the Synoptic Gospels does Jesus suggest that he intends to radically depart from Judaism and create a church.

In addressing a largely Gentile population Paul avoids using the term Messiah thus circumventing any Judaic and nationalistic expectation. Rather he refers to Jesus as *Kyrios,* Lord or *Christos* which almost becomes a surname as in Jesus Christ. Paul's teaching has already been discussed. Paul's faith was in the Risen Lord. Jesus had acted on God's behalf to overcome the powers of sin, death and evil. Jesus 'humbled himself and became obedient unto death, even death on a cross' (Phil. 2.8).

As consequence, 'Is it Christ Jesus, who died, yes, who was raised from the dead, who is at the right hand of God, who indeed intercedes for us?' (Rom. 8.34).

Paul had great expectations for the future of Christianity, 'At the name of Jesus every knee should bow, in heaven and on earth and under the earth, and every tongue confess that Jesus Christ is Lord' (Phil. 2.10).

Paul believed that this was imminent and would happen suddenly, 'For you yourselves know well that the day of the Lord [second coming] will come like a thief in the night' (1 Thes. 5.2). Paul's conviction that Jesus was alive and in him meant that he could speak of 'Christ living in us' (Gal. 2.20) or that, 'You are the body of Christ and individually members of it' (1 Cor. 12.27). The concept was of a new humanity.

In the Gospel of John, on the other hand, Jesus is acknowledged to be the Christ from the very beginning of his public ministry (1.41, 49). Only once does Jesus explicitly claim to be the Messiah.

The woman said to him, 'I know that Messiah is coming (he who is called Christ); when he comes, he will show us all things.' Jesus said to her, 'I who speak to you am he.' (John 4.25–26).

According to John, Jesus never attempted to conceal that he was the Messiah. At the feast of the Dedication in Jerusalem he was questioned by Jews about his status and he replied, 'I told you and you do not believe.' As a consequence they threatened to stone Jesus and subsequently attempted to arrest him but he escaped.

We do not know to what extent the authors of the New Testament were influenced by being committed members of a new religion as they wrote their accounts of the life of Jesus. Faced with this contradictory evidence we are unable to tell for certain whether or not Jesus believed that he was the Messiah as expected by the Jews. According to the Synoptic Gospels Jesus never asserted directly or spontaneously that he was the Messiah. Christian apologists often suggest that he believed that he was the Messiah but not as the Jews expected. Then why allow them to live under a misconception? Did he not regard his task to simply announce the impending intervention of God in some mysterious way to establish a new world order? Even after his resurrection, his disciples continued to believe in the traditional concept of a Messiah because they ask him, 'Lord, will you at this time restore the kingdom to Israel?' (Acts 1.6).

Son of God

The title 'Son of God' is most frequently given to Jesus in the writings of John, Paul and in the letter to the Hebrews. The implication of the title to a casual reader would be to infer a divine nature to Jesus. The early Church fathers would develop the concept of him being of the same substance of God and thus equal.

In the Bible the expression 'son of God' is not confined to Jesus alone. Angels are regarded as sons of God (Job 1.6; 38.7; Ps, 29.1; Daniel 3.25). The king is occasionally called God's son,

'I will be his father, and he shall be my son' (2 Sam. 7.14) and 'I have set my king on Zion, my holy hill. I will tell of the decree of the Lord: He said to me, "You are my son, today I have begotten you"' (Ps. 2.6–7; 89.26–27).

Israelites are described as God's son: 'Israel is my son, my first-born' (Exodus 4.22).

'When Israel was a child, then I loved him, and called my son out of Egypt' (Hos. 11.1).

Pharaoh was told, 'Let my son go, that he may serve me' (Exod. 4.23).

Finally, righteous men are called sons of God: 'Be like a father to orphans, and as good as a husband to widows. And you will be like a son to the Most High, whose love of you will surpass your mother's' (Ecclesiasticus 4.10 JB).

'If the virtuous man is God's son, God will take his part and rescue him from the clutches of his enemies' (Wisdom 2.18 JB).

In Deuteronomy we read:

If you obey the voice of the Lord your God, keeping all his commandments which I command you this day, and doing right in the sight of the Lord your God. You are the sons of the Lord your God (Deut, 13.18; 14.1).

With the dubious exception of the angels, the general thrust of the argument is that the righteous become sons of God by adoption. In the Old Testament, 'son of God' is a figure of speech as they could not conceive of a human being literally divine. Classical Hellenistic mythology depicting children born of a union of Olympian gods and earthly women was an anathema to Judaism.

The use of 'son of God' to describe Jesus is to say the least, ambiguous. It is helpful to consider the expression in the context in which it was used. The most common was when Jesus was portrayed as a charismatic exorcist or miracle worker. On one occasion Jesus had healed many by the laying on of hands and exorcism:

And whenever the unclean spirits beheld him, they fell down before him and cried out, 'Thou are the son of God.' And he strictly ordered them not to make him known (Mark 3.11, 12; Luke 4.41).

It was common practice after exorcism to command, 'be silent' but why keep his status secret? Did Jesus disagree with them or was he uncertain about his status? Was this a tactical ploy to defer knowledge of his status? On this event alone no conclusion is certain. In the region of the Gerasenes a man possessed by a demon called Legion begs Jesus to leave him in peace: 'What have you to do with me, Jesus, son of the Most High God? I adjure you by God, do not torment me.' (Mark 5.7; Matthew 8.29; Luke 8.28) These are demonic voices but whilst Jesus is in the wilderness, Satan tempts him with similar words, 'If you are the Son of God, command these stones to become loaves of bread', and then, 'If you are the Son of God, throw yourself down [from the pinnacle of the temple]' (Matthew 4.3–6; Luke 4.3–10). It is after another miraculous occurrence, namely Jesus walking on the Lake of Galilee, the disciples declare, 'Truly you are the Son of God' (Matthew 14.33). These examples describe Jesus as the Son of God by virtue of him being a miracle worker.

On two significant occasions, Jesus' baptism and transfiguration, there is apparent confirmation of Jesus as son of God. Once Jesus had been baptized:

Immediately he saw the heavens opened and the Spirit descending upon him like a dove; and a voice came from heaven, 'Thou art my beloved Son; with thee I am well pleased' (Mark 1.10–11; Luke 3.22; Matthew 3.17).

On another occasion, Jesus took Peter, James and John up a high mountain where he was transfigured with his garments intensely white and glistening. Elijah and Moses appeared with them.

And a cloud overshadowed them, and a voice came out of the cloud, 'This is my beloved Son; listen to him' (Mark 9.7; Luke 9.35). Matthew (17.5) inserts 'with whom I am well pleased'.

Following his baptismal experience when a voice described him as 'my beloved Son' perhaps Jesus would reciprocate by referring to God as 'my Father' using the Aramaic word 'Abba'. Whilst in the garden of Gethsemane Jesus prays, 'Abba, Father, all things are possible to thee; remove this cup from me; yet not what I will, but what thou wilt' (Mark 14.36). When his disciples ask to be taught how to pray, Jesus says, 'Father, hallowed be thy name, Thy kingdom come' (Luke 11.2). The early church used the same formula, 'And because you are sons, God has sent the Spirit of his Son into your heart, crying, "Abba! Father!"' (Gal. 4.6). The use of 'Abba' could reflect Jesus' own consciousness of an immediate and intimate contact with his heavenly Father. It could also indicate an awareness of his special status. However, Jesus taught his disciples to address their prayers to *our* Father. This would suggest that Jesus did not consider his relationship to God was unique but was attainable by others.

Two verses in the Synoptic Gospels deserve mention.

All things have been delivered to me by my Father; and no one knows the Son except the Father, and no one knows the Father except the Son and any one to whom the Son chooses to reveal him (Matthew 11.27; Luke 10.22).

Speaking about the kingdom of God, Jesus says, 'But of that day or that hour no one knows, not even the angels in heaven, nor the Son; but only the Father' (Mark 13.32; Matt. 24.36). These are the only references in the Synoptic Gospels where Jesus himself implies that he is the Son of God.

The title 'Son of God' must have been transmitted outside Jesus' circle of close followers. As Jesus hung on the cross, passers-by derided him saying, 'If you are the Son of God come down from the cross'. Chief priests and elders mocked him, 'He saved others; he cannot save himself. He is the King of Israel; let

193

him come down now from the cross, and we will believe him. He trusts in God; let God deliver him now, if he desires him; for he said, "I am the Son of God."' (Matthew 27.39–43).

As Jesus dies and an earthquake shakes the land the centurion and others declare, 'Truly this was a Son of God!' (Matthew 27.54; Mark 15.39).

Whether or not Jesus saw himself as the Messiah or the Son of God is doubtful on the evidence in the Synoptic Gospels. Whilst these titles are occasionally attributed to Jesus he never elaborates on their meaning. It was Paul and particularly John who developed the concept of God incarnate most fully. Paul, writing to the Galatians explains,

> But when the time had fully come, God sent forth his Son, born of a woman, born under the law, to redeem those who were under the law, so that we might receive adoption as sons (Gal. 4.4–5).

John avoids using the title 'Son of God'. He would have been aware that in the Hellenistic culture great achievements were interpreted as divine manifestations. An Asian inscription of 48 BC speaks of Julius Caesar as 'god manifest, offspring of Ares and Aphrodite, and common saviour of human life'. A marble pedestal from Pergamum bears the inscription, 'The Emperor Caesar, son of God, god Augustus, overseer of land and sea'. Jesus could not be described as the Son of God with its Hellenistic connotation.

John's Use of "the Word" or "Logos"

John's gospel opens with the words:

> In the beginning was the Word, and the Word was with God, and the Word was God. He was in the beginning with God; all things were made through him, and without him was not anything made that was mad.

It is one of best known passages in the New Testament but often misunderstood in today's culture. To John's audience at the time the message would have resonated as a new but believable concept. It was a clear message that required no explanation. A diversion into Greek culture is necessary at this point.

To understand the context of John's opening words, another text is helpful.

To his Logos [Word], his chief messenger, highest in age and honour, the Father of all has given the special prerogative to stand on the border and separate the creature from the Creator. This same Logos both pleads with the Immortal as suppliant for afflicted mortality and acts as ambassador of the ruler to the subject. He glories in this prerogative and proudly describes it in these words: 'I stood between the Lord and you.' (Quoted in Fredriksen, 1988, p.9).

This could be read in a Christian pulpit today and the congregation would concur with this description of the Messiah. However, the author was Philo Judeas, leader of the Jews living in Alexandria c. 20 BC to 45 AD. He was thus a contemporary of John the Baptist, Jesus and the most distinguished Pharisee, Hillel. His intellectual background was quite different as he subscribed to the philosophy of Plato in its various forms. Philo's work was an attempt to reconcile Judaism and Platonism. He wrote a large number of commentaries on Genesis and Exodus, which transformed them into allegories of divine *logos* (reason). He endorsed Plato's belief that there was more to a story than its literal meaning. The timeless dimension of reality was more real than its physical or historical dimension. He was seeking a more fundamental level of truth, a process he called *hyponoia*, or higher/deeper thought. To take one simple example, Philo argued that the world may not have been made in literally six days, but rather that it reflected perfection as at that time six was a symbol of perfection.

Philo also refined the biblical concept of God, which could seem hopelessly anthropomorphic to a Platonist. The Bible, in common with all the great transcendental philosophers of classical antiquity, had assumed that above all there was a single indivisible self-sufficient principle; and although they might call it (him) sometimes God, sometimes Monad (Pythagorean), sometimes Absolute Beauty or the Idea of the Good (Plato's *Phaedrus* and *Republic*), sometimes the Unmoved Mover or Self-thinking Thought (Aristotle's *Metaphysics*), they were all agreed that it was single. Moreover, there was a general acceptance of Plato's view that one should differentiate between God's *ousia*, his essence, which was entirely incomprehensible to human beings, and his activities (*energeiaei*) and powers (*dynamies*) that we can apprehend in the world. Philo believed that there was nothing about God's *ousia* in the scripture; we only read about his powers, one of which was the Word or Logos of God, the rational design that structures the universe.

The early Christian evangelists' prime argument for their faith was that Jesus' life and death had been predicted by the Hebrew prophets, an argument that the Romans, with their respect for augury and oracles, took very seriously. Once Marconion had urged Christians to jettison the Hebrew scriptures, some Gentile converts became uncertain about their beliefs and the relevance of their Jewish heritage. They were no longer members of the synagogue. Christians began writing *apologiae* or rational explanations of their faith. One of the earliest of these apologists was Justin (100–160 AD), a pagan convert from Samaria who eventually died as a martyr. The *logos* in the prologue to John's gospel reminded him of the fiery, divine breath that the Stoics believed organised the whole of reality and called *Logos* (Reason), *Pneuma* (Spirit) or God. Justin argued that Jesus was the incarnation of the Logos, which had been active in the world throughout history, inspiring Greeks and Hebrews alike. It had spoken through the prophets, who had thus been able to foretell the coming of the Messiah. It had spoken through Plato and Socrates. When Moses thought he heard God speaking from the burning bush, he had really been listening to the Logos. It is in this context we should read John's exposition of Christian belief that Jesus was the incarnation of the Word or Logos and admire his genius for assimilating different traditions into a readily understood form at the time.

Both Philo and John were writing in a world dominated by Greek culture. Philo was attempting to explain God's intervention in the world as recorded in Hebrew Scriptures. John had God's ultimate intervention in the person of Jesus. What is surprising is the number of similarities between these two great thinkers who were able to interpret both Jewish and Christian belief as being compatible with the Greek culture appertaining at that time. The history of Christianity is that of constant reinterpretation of scriptures with changing circumstances.

John gives a radical change in the portrayal of Jesus from the Synoptic Gospels. The emphasis is now on Jesus himself:

> For God so loved the world that he gave his only Son, that whoever believes in him should not perish but have eternal life. For God sent the Son into the world, not to condemn the world, but that the world might be saved through him (3.16–17).

The concept of God incarnate became one of the cardinal beliefs of Christianity.

Differing Beliefs in the Early Church

The problem is that the New Testament scriptures are not as clear or as unambiguous as many fundamentalists believe. Once John states the full divinity of Jesus as, 'I and my Father are one' (10:30) we have to reconcile it with Mark's Jesus saying, 'Why callest thou me good? There is none good but one, that is God' (10.18). It is not surprising that the early church was divided into numerous sects. In the Corinthian church Paul had a stormy relationship with another Christian missionary, Apollos. The church was divided, 'For when one says, "I belong to Paul", and another, "I belong to Apollos", are you not merely men?' (1 Corinthians 1.12).

Apollos came from Samaria, hence Paul's reference to him as Hebrew rather than Judean. He had probably been converted

197

to Christianity by Philip on his missionary journey to Samaria. His cultural background differed from the Jews. Samaritans believed that the sacred texts were confined to the Pentateuch and the book of Joshua; they worshipped in the tabernacle rather than in the Temple and had no concept of life after death. Apollos' main emphasis was on wisdom and knowledge as the primary fruits of conversion rather than faith and love. These were the seeds of Gnosticism that were later to flourish. In the first three chapters of his first letter to the Corinthians Paul attacks such views.

> Christ did not send me to… preach with eloquent
> wisdom… I will destroy the wisdom of the wise, and the
> understanding of the understanding I will thwart. Where is
> the wise man?... Has not God made foolish the wisdom of
> the world? … I did not come proclaiming to you the
> testimony of God in lofty words or wisdom… my speech and
> my message were not in plausible words of wisdom (1 Cor.
> 1.17, 19, 20; 2.1, 4).

It is difficult to believe that such language would impress Gentiles with a Hellenistic background. Paul must have recognised this and his second letter to the Corinthians is very different in tone. To give just a few examples, 'Now you excel in everything – in faith, in utterances, in knowledge' (8.7); 'We destroy arguments and every proud obstacle to the knowledge of God' (10.5); 'Even if I am unskilled in speaking, I am not in knowledge' (11.6). By the time Paul writes to the Colossians and the Ephesians he has fully embraced the importance of knowledge and wisdom, 'To have all the riches of assured understanding and the knowledge of God's mystery' (Col. 2.2); '[You] have put on the new nature, which is being renewed in knowledge after the image of its creator' (Col. 3.10); 'Let the word of Christ dwell in you richly, as you teach and admonish one another in all wisdom' (Col. 3.16); and, 'For he has made known to us in all wisdom and insight the mystery of his will' (Eph. 1.9). This becomes a central theme in John's gospel written about four decades later.

Apollos has been used simply as an example of the profound doctrinal differences that existed in the early church and the emerging theology. What is clear is that the early church was not united in 'one faith' but there were many interpretations on the life of Jesus. This was reflected in the numerous accounts of the life of Jesus that were not included in the canon of the New Testament. More significantly there were differing schools of thought. The Docetists believed that Jesus' body was only apparently human. Ebonites stressed the humanity of Jesus and denied his divinity. Adoptionists probably predate Mark's gospel. They believed that Jesus was adopted as God's son at his baptism because of his sinless devotion to the will of God. Marcionites believed that Jesus was the saviour sent by God and that Paul of Tarsus was his chief apostle but rejected the Old Testament and the God of Israel. They believed that the wrathful Hebrew God was a separate and lower entity than the all-forgiving God of the New Testament.

Another prominent group of Christians were the Gnostics (derived from the Greek for 'knowledge'). Much of what we know of the Gnostics is the result of a discovery in 1945 at Nag Hammadi on the west bank of the Nile about eighty kilometres north of Luxor. Two Egyptian brothers whilst digging for fertiliser found a sealed earthenware jar containing thirteen leather-bound papyrus codices. They date back to the second-century AD and are mostly Gnostic texts. They were probably buried when such texts were banned after the council at Nicea. The contents were made public in 1975. Their emphasis was not so much to believe in Jesus, as John's Gospel emphasises, but to seek to know God through one's own, divinely given capacity, since all are created in the image of God. God's light shines not only in Jesus but potentially at least, in everyone. There is much mysticism in some of the texts. Those who discover God in themselves, and themselves in God transform gnosis into action. To quote from The Gospel of Truth, sometimes attributed to Valentinus:

Speak the truth to those who seek it,
And speak of understanding to those who have

Committed sin through error;
Strengthen the feet of those who have stumbled;
Extend your hands those who are sick;
Feed those who are hungry;
Give rest to those who are weary;
And raise up those who wish to rise (Quoted in
Pagels, 2003, p. 122).

Arius argued that Christ as the Son of God did not always exist but was created by God. In other words he was distinct from God and inferior to him. Athanasius, a companion of the Bishop of Alexandria, regarded this as heretical and dangerous to the salvation of souls. God's attributes are eternal including his Fatherhood. Thus, the Father was always the Father, and the son always existed with him. He believed that the Son was of the *same substance* as the Father, co-eternal with him.

With such divergent views a consensus of opinion was desirable. This was attempted at the Council of Nicea in 325 AD which is the subject of the next chapter.

XIII

Reflections on the Nicene Creed

The Roman Emperor Constantine I (272–377 AD) was the foremost general of his time controlling Britain, Gaul and Spain. His mother, Helena, was a Christian. In 312 AD he confronted his main rival, Maxentius, at the battle at the Milvian Bridge just north of Rome. Prior to the battle he either had a dream or saw a cross arising from the light of the sun carrying the message, 'In this sign you will conquer'. He gave orders that the imperial standard and the soldiers' shields be decorated with the Christian symbol consisting of a Chi (X) traversed by a Rho (P) representing the first two Greek letters for Christos. Although his army was half the size of Maxentius', he was victorious and attributed victory to the power of God of the Christians. Nevertheless he celebrated with a triumphal arch, the Arch of Constantine, in Rome with references to Apollo, Diana and Hercules but no Christian symbol.

The most severe persecution of Christians in Roman history occurred in 303 AD under the orders of Diocletian. In 313 AD Constantine was a co-author of the Edict of Milan allowing toleration of all religions throughout the empire. In 325 AD he convened a meeting of the church leaders at Nicea, now Iznik in modern Turkey, to agree a common doctrine. Between 250 and 318 bishops each with two priests and three deacons attended. As previously mentioned, Arius argued that Christ as the Son of God did not always exist but was created by God. In other words, he was distinct from God and inferior to him. Athanasius, a companion of the Bishop of Alexandria, regarded this as heretical and dangerous to the salvation of souls. God's attributes

201

are eternal, including his Fatherhood. Thus, the Father was always the father, and that the son always existed with him. He believed that the Son was of the *same substance* as the Father, co-eternal with him. Both arguments could be supported by quotations from scripture but as mentioned in the introduction, doctrine is not entirely dependent on scriptures. It is probable that each proponent's different pattern of worship and sense of personal salvation featured in the argument.

After a month of bitter debate, Athanasius carried the day and the Nicene Creed was accepted by all except for two dissenters. Three key phrases are worthy of mention. Jesus is described as 'God from God, Light from Light, true God from true God', signifying his divinity (Nicene Creed 1988 ecumenical translation). Jesus is described as 'begotten, not made' asserting his co-eternality with God and his role in creation. The Greek *homoousios* or of the same substance is translated as 'consubstantial' or 'one in being with the Father'.

Constantine's motivation for calling the council is open to speculation but he would no doubt have believed that a Roman Empire united by one common faith would have been a much more potent force in the world. The Emperor was not involved in the doctrinal debate but once agreement had been reached those who refused to endorse the Creed were exiled and excommunicated, including Arius. His works were to be confiscated and burnt and those persons found possessing them were to be executed. Nevertheless, Arianism continued to be a significant cause of dissention until the eighth century. The doctrine of the Trinity and of God incarnate was thus firmly established and remains the core of Christian belief.

Constantine became a patron for the Christian faith. He supported the Church financially, endowed it with land and other wealth, built numerous basilicas, promoted Christians to high-ranking offices and granted privileges to the clergy. Between 324 and 330 AD, Constantine built a new imperial capital at Byzantium on the Bosphorus in which worship was confined to Christian churches. The city was later renamed Constantinople. However, Constantine remained torn between the Arian and Trinitarian camps. He later recalled Arius from exile and banished Athanasius. Just before his death in 337 AD, he was baptized by the Arian Bishop Eusebius of Nicodemia.

Today the Nicene Creed is used in the liturgy of almost all Christian Churches. Another creed that is widely used is the Apostles' Creed, based on the old Roman Creed that probably predates the Nicene Creed. The Apostles' Creed in its present form dates from the early eighth century. It does not explicitly address some of the Christological issues such as the divinity of either Jesus or of the Holy Spirit. It is common practice to use the Nicene Creed during celebration of the Eucharist or the Holy Communion and the Apostles' Creed at Baptisms. History is written by the victors and our knowledge of the alternative interpretations of the role of Jesus has largely disappeared and is now classified as heresy.

Apostle's Creed

This is included simply as a point of reference as used in the Church of England's *Book of Common Prayer*:

I believe in God the Father Almighty,
Maker of heaven and earth.

And in Jesus Christ his only Son our Lord,
Who was conceived by the Holy Ghost,
Born of the Virgin Mary,
Suffered under Pontius Pilate,
Was crucified, dead, and buried:
He descended into hell;
The third day he rose again from the dead;
He ascended into heaven,
And sitteth on the right hand of God the Father Almighty;
From thence he shall come to judge the quick and the dead.

I believe in the Holy Ghost;
The holy Catholick Church;
The Communion of Saints;
The Forgiveness of sins;

The Resurrection of the body,
And the Life everlasting.
Amen.

Reading the Nicene Creed

In discussing the Nicene Creed, the 1988 ecumenical translation is used:

We believe in one God, the Father, the Almighty, maker of heaven and earth, of all that is, seen and unseen.

All theists would agree with these opening words. The use of the word almighty may be misconstrued. The religious person turns in his distress to the power of God in the world and uses him as a *Deus ex machina* or a puppeteer pulling the strings from above. It deliberately contradicts the Docetists who thought that God was too perfect to create a world of natural disasters, suffering and sin.

I believe in one Lord, Jesus Christ, the only son of God, eternally begotten of the Father, God from God, Light from Light, true God from true God, begotten, not made, of one being with the Father; through him all things were made.

Previous discussion has thrown doubt on whether Jesus thought of himself in these terms. 'Eternally begotten of the Father' is an attack on Arius who believed that Jesus was begat or created by God and prior to this did not exist. In the Creed Jesus represented not an event in time but an eternal relationship. God was Father and as such had always been Father. Any suggestion that Jesus was in any way inferior to God is dismissed. The Catholic Latin Rite uses 'consubstantial with the Father' rather than 'of one being' both being representations of the Greek *homoousious.* It is improbable that Paul in describing Jesus as 'being in the form of God' (Phillip 2.6) thought of him as 'of one being.' The debate has continued over the centuries and remains one of the mysteries of faith.

For us and for our salvation He came down from heaven, was incarnate of the Holy Spirit and the Virgin Mary and became truly human.

If the chapter on the Incarnation has any rationale, then this is at best 'poetic language'. Nestorius, Archbishop of Constantinople from 428 to 431 AD, reignited the debate. He rejected the long-used title of Mother of God for the Virgin Mary as it venerated her almost as a goddess. Nestorius believed that no union between the human and the divine were possible. If such a union of human and divine occurred, Nestorius believed that Christ could not truly be con-substantial with God and con-substantial with us because he would grow, mature, suffer and die (which he said God cannot do) and also possess the power of God that would separate him from being equal to humans. At the First Council of Ephesus in 431 AD he was deposed and declared a heretic.

For our sake he was crucified under Pontius Pilate; He suffered death and was buried.

There can be no doubt about his crucifixion and death. The preceding clause includes, 'for our salvation' repeated here as 'for our sake'. This was readily comprehensible in a culture where sacrifice to the gods was a part of everyday life. The concept of atonement is more difficult to understand in the twenty-first century. This has been discussed in chapter eleven and remains one of the mysteries of Christian faith.

On the third day he rose again in accordance with the Scriptures.

In spite of the empty tomb it does not appear that Jesus was a resuscitated corpse rather he was a 'body of Spirit'. He is described appearing to his close companions in varying forms. All that we can be certain about is that his disciples were convinced that he was still present with them and his power continued to enable them to cast out demons and heal the sick.

He ascended into heaven and is seated at the right hand of the Father. He will come in glory to judge the living and the dead, and his kingdom will have no end.

As has been discussed, Jesus' ascension is portrayed in different ways in the Gospels. This is picture language to explain why Jesus was no longer visible based on the three tier view of the universe; heaven above a flat earth and hell below. In the time of Paul many Christians expected Jesus to return within their lifetime and this reiterates their hope. Jesus spoke of the kingdom of God in terms that his audience understood as the fulfilment of Old Testament prophesy. This now becomes the kingdom of Jesus Christ and its meaning is vague. This may be a kingdom in heaven for souls that have been saved or it may be a kingdom on earth. There are no unequivocal answers in the New Testament.

We believe in the Holy Spirit, the Lord, the giver of
Life, who proceeds from the Father and the Son,
who with the Father and the Son is worshipped and
glorified,who has spoken through the prophets.

This includes the most controversial phrase, 'from the Father and the Son'. This is the main doctrinal difference between Eastern and Western churches and is known as the Filioque controversy. The phrase was not in the original Creed but added later to stress that the Son was not less than his Father. It was declared true by Pope Leo 1 in 447 AD. The Eastern Church maintained that the Holy Spirit was not inferior to the Son and could not have 'proceeded from the Son'. It is beyond the scope of this book to address the issue but much of the controversy arises from different nuances in the Latin and Greek texts. Three Lambeth Conferences (1888, 1978 and 1988) representing the Anglican Churches have recommended that the phrase be dropped as a measure of ecumenical understanding. For the Roman Catholic Church to drop the clause would amount to a reversal of established dogma.

In general, the authors of the Old Testament avoid using the anthropomorphic phrase, 'God did this or that'. Rather they speak of the Spirit, Word or Wisdom of God intervening as in, 'By the word of the Lord the heavens were made, and all their host by the breath of his mouth' (Psalm. 33.6). Thus it is the Spirit of God that makes Joseph a skilled ruler (Genesis 41.38), Joshua a military genius (Numbers 27.18) or Samuel an ecstatic prophet (1 Sam. 10.6, 10).

In the New Testament the terminology changes from the Spirit of God to the Holy Spirit as a distinct entity. The Virgin birth is attributed to the Holy Spirit (Matthew 1.18, 20) and Jesus' baptism is blessed by the Holy Spirit (Luke 3.22). Otherwise there are few references to the Holy Spirit in the Gospels prior to Jesus' ascension to heaven. John (7.39) explains that, 'For as yet the Spirit had not been given, because Jesus was not yet glorified'. On the other hand the Creed says that the Holy Spirit has spoken through the prophets. Jesus promises his disciples:

These things I have spoken to you, while I am still with you. But the Counsellor, the Holy Spirit, whom the Father will send in my name, he will teach you all things, and bring to your remembrance all that I have said to you (John 14.25–26).

Similarly in Mark, Jesus says:

And when they bring you to trial and deliver you up, do not be anxious beforehand what you are to say; but say whatever is given to you in that hour, for it is not you who speak, but the Holy Spirit (Mark 13.11).

Luke's phraseology is even more affirmative:

Settle it therefore in your minds, not to meditate beforehand how to answer; for I will give you a mouth and wisdom, which none of your adversaries will be able to withstand or contradict (Luke 21.14–15).

In Luke's highly symbolic account, the Holy Spirit descends on the disciples on the Feast of Pentecost. This was the anniversary of Moses receiving the Ten Commandments on Mount Sinai; the Old Covenant. The Holy Spirit conveyed the New Covenant. Luke regards the speaking with tongues (glossolalia) as unmistakable sign of the gift of the Holy Spirit (Acts 2.1–4). After forty years in the wilderness Moses was taken up ('assumed') to heaven. After forty days of post-resurrection appearances, Jesus is taken up to heaven. Luke develops the analogy further in Stephen's speech in his own defence (Acts 7).

John's account is rather different. Early on the Sunday morning Jesus appears to Mary Magdalene and that evening to the disciples in a closed room and breathed on them, and said to them, 'Receive the Holy Spirit' (John 20.22).

The New Testament formulates no doctrine of the Trinity. The early church considered itself to be living in the latter days in expectation of the coming kingdom of God. Before the death of Jesus the Holy Spirit was unknown to the disciples, although John records Jesus telling them about the future sending of the Holy Spirit (John 14.16–18). The Christian religion is largely dependent on the intensity of the conviction of the disciples that the Holy Spirit had descended on them during the feast of Pentecost. This was incorporated into their liturgy. It is inconceivable that Jesus actually said, 'Go therefore and make disciples of all nations, baptizing them in the name of the Father and of the Son and of the Holy Spirit' (Matthew 28.19). As part of the liturgy it would have been reasonable to attribute these words to Jesus but such language is not reflected in the other teachings of Jesus.

We believe in one holy catholic and apostolic church.
We acknowledge one baptism for the forgiveness of sins.

This reflected the belief of the Christian community. Many would regard the term 'catholic' as meaning universal as there are now over three thousand different denominations in the Church. Baptism was a new ceremony introduced by John the

Baptist adapted from the Jewish tradition of ritual bathing prior to entering the Temple. The practice of baptizing seriously ill newborn infants for the forgiveness of their sins lacks any rational or ethical basis.

We look for the resurrection of the dead and the life of the world to come.

These are articles of faith. The Creed avoids a phrase used in the earlier Apostles' Creed that is still extensively used. This speaks of the resurrection of the body and reflects Matthew's description of what happened at the moment of Jesus' death. 'The earth shook, and the rocks were split; the tombs also were opened, and many bodies of the saints who had fallen asleep were raised, and coming out of the tombs after his resurrection they went into the holy city and appeared to many' (Matthew 27.51–53).

The Creed officially placed Jesus on a plane synonymous with God. All other interpretations of the life of Jesus were regarded as heretical. With constant repetition in the liturgy of the church it inevitably became sacrosanct and beyond question. It is worth speculating as to what Jesus would have thought of the Nicene Creed. He would have agreed with the first and last sentences, but would he have recognised himself in the rest of the Creed? Even Paul uses more refrained language in describing Jesus as being the likeness of God (2 Corinthians 4.4) or 'He is the image of the invisible God' (1 Collosians 1.15). The Creed derives its origin in part from an interpretation of the Gospel by Christians influenced by the world of Hellenism and particularly John's unique exegesis of the significances of Jesus. The Creed says nothing about the teachings of Jesus. It is a document that defines Jesus to being equal to God thus rejecting all alternative interpretations of his life that were current at the time. There are no references to moral or ethical values and consequently has little relevance to human behaviour.

It is not surprising that following a union of church and state, the church would emulate many of the functions of state. Power, wealth and authority would gravitate to the centre in Rome.

Constantine's legalisation of Christianity has resulted in political and theological changes, described as the Constantinian shift. This has had a profound influence on the nature of Christianity that reverberates to this day.

Conclusion

Christians, irrespective of their denominational allegiance, have found comfort and strength through their faith. This they find in varying degrees through scriptures, the sacraments, prayers and hymns. They believe that Jesus is still active in their lives and the dedication of many is extraordinary. This book represents an attempt to understand the origin of those beliefs that underlie their faith. The New Testament reveals a gradual development in various author's different interpretations of the life of Jesus. This may be summarised by first considering the Synoptic Gospels then Paul of Tarsus and finally John.

The Synoptic Gospels

These were written forty to seventy years after the death of Jesus and inevitably they would have to acknowledge the significant changes that had occurred in the intervening time. A largely Gentile church had been established, arguably contrary to the expectations of Jesus. The Temple in Jerusalem had been totally destroyed. Christians were being persecuted. Jesus' main message was to repent as the kingdom of God was at hand. God would intervene in some dramatic way to create a new world order. As this was imminent he taught his followers not to worry about tomorrow, not to secure wealth and to accept current temporal powers such as Caesar. He despises work and the duties of family life. Jesus' teaching on the Judaic hope for their kingdom of God has not materialised as a temporal reality and the Christian community has gradually reinterpreted the concept.

Perhaps the least reliable historical details concern Jesus' trial. Under the threat of persecution it was necessary to exonerate Pontius Pilate and hold the Jews entirely responsible for his death. The only credible account of Jesus' crucifixion is in John's gospel. There was no trial; it was a summary execution agreed between the high priest Caiaphas and Pontius Pilate. This occurred on the afternoon before the Passover supper. The roots of anti-Semitism are reinforced in the Synoptic Gospels. Christians should question their uncritical acceptance of these accounts and the consequent horrors. After all, Jesus was a Jew. At times, the authors would attribute words to Jesus that reflected the changed circumstances but of questionable validity.

Paul of Tarsus

Paul was a man with unbounded energy, immense courage and vision. His great contribution was to take the message of Jesus to the Gentile world. Without Paul the followers of Jesus would probably have remained a sect within Judaism worshipping in the Temple. He was convinced that Jesus had revealed himself on the road to Damascus. Paul believed that he was living in the last days of the world and Jesus would return in his lifetime. Later he became convinced that Christians were experiencing the kingdom of God as they 'walked in the newness of life'. Paul had no knowledge or interest in Jesus' life on earth. As a consequence there are paradoxes in his teaching that have become embedded in Christianity today.

John

John had the ability to elevate Jesus to a figure to be worshipped alongside God. He did this by assimilating Greek philosophy into his gospel thus making it more comprehensible to the Gentile world. This is not to deride his work as this has been the history of the Christian church over two millennia. The Christian message has gradually changed to incorporate newer concepts of the universe and social justice to name but two. However, it is important to understand the New Testament as an evolving human understanding of the nature and significance of Jesus. It was John who created the concept of Jesus as incarnate and divine that is the cornerstone of Christian belief. Jesus was a Jew who never contemplated a new religion but emphasised the spiritual core of Judaism and its expectation for the imminent kingdom of God. This has not materialised as a temporal reality. It was the creativity of Paul of Tarsus and John that gave birth to Christian belief.

To conclude, I can do no better than affirm three quotations. Albert Schweitzer in his book *The Quest of the Historical Jesus* he quotes Hartmann who wrote:

> When He felt His death was drawing nigh He struck the balance of His life, found His mission a failure, His person and His cause abandoned by God, and died with the unanswered question on His lips, 'My God why hast thou forsaken me?' (Schweitzer, 2005, p.319).

Although this is often quoted in isolation, Schweitzer wrote in his last chapter:

> But the truth is, it is not Jesus as historically known, but Jesus as spiritually arisen within men, who is significant for our time. Not the historical Jesus, but the spirit which goes forth from Him and in the spirits of men strives for new influence and rule, is that which overcomes the world (Schweitzer, 2005, p.399).

This is the experience of many Christians today who desire a better world. This is fostered by communal worship including the sacraments, hymn singing and the fellowship of others. However, the belief that Christian doctrine is entirely based on the historical Jesus is unsustainable.

Richard Holloway was Bishop of Edinburgh and Primus of the Scottish Episcopal Church until 2000, and Gresham Professor of Divinity until 2001. His book, *Godless Morality* states:

> The use of God in any moral debate is so problematic as to be almost worthless. We can debate with one another as to

whether this or that alleged claim genuinely emanated from God, but who can honestly adjudicate in such an Olympian dispute? That is why it is better to leave God out of the moral debate and find good human reasons for supporting the system or approach we advocate, without having recourse to divinely clinching arguments (Holloway, 2004, p.20).

He further states:

If we have become persuaded that a particular claim is not true or is one we can no longer hold with a clear conscience, then we are making a moral judgment; we are saying that it is important to act on what we believe to be true and not cling to falsehoods because they comfort us or because they have beneficial secondary effects (Holloway, 2004, p.3).

Maurice Casey in *From Jewish Prophet to Gentile God* concludes:

If churches as organisations must insist on false beliefs we can always leave them, and follow from outside their orbit those aspects of the teaching of Jesus which we judge relevant to our lives 2,000 years later (Casey, 1991, p. 178).

However, such a stark choice is easier said than done. Many Christians, irrespective of their denominational allegiances, have a similar childhood background to the lady mentioned at the beginning of this book who wished she'd been brought up as a Lutheran or my own background as a son of the Manse. We almost automatically entered a likeminded community in which we felt comfortable. Others with different backgrounds have decided to join such communities. Undoubtedly, there remains a strong desire to remain part of that fellowship even when one has intellectual reservations. Such behaviour is not unique to religious organisations. An analogy can be found in the world of politics. In 1961 the United States of America invaded Cuba with the intention of deposing the communist leader, Fidel Castro.

The landing site was the Bay of Pigs. It proved to be a disaster with a humiliating defeat of the American troops. Charles Handy in *Understanding Organisations* wrote:

'How could we have been so stupid?' asked President John F. Kennedy, after he and a group of close advisers had blundered into the Bay of Pigs invasion.

Stupidity was certainly not the explanation. The group who made the decision was one of the greatest collections of intellectual talent in the history of American government. Irving Janis describes the blunder as a result of 'group-think'.

Group-think occurs when too high a price is placed on the harmony and morale of the group, so that loyalty to the group's previous policies, or to the group consensus, overrides the conscience of each member. 'Concurrence-seeking' drives out the realistic appraisal of alternatives. No bickering or conflict is allowed to spoil the cosy 'we-feeling' of the group. Thus it is that even the cleverest, most high-minded and well-intentioned of people can get into a blind spot... The result of group-think is that the group looks at too few alternatives, is insensitive to the risks in its favourite strategy, finds it hard to rethink a strategy that is failing and becomes very selective in the sort of facts it sees and asks for. Group-think is unfortunately most rife at the top and centre of organizations where the need for 'keeping things close' seems more important...

Kennedy learnt his lesson. The Missile Crisis was handled differently, with a more diffuse group, more outside ideas, more testing of alternatives and more sensitivity to conflicting ideas (Handy, 1993, p.163).

Once 'group think' becomes the norm, members become reluctant to express their doubts publicly for fear of derision or exclusion. Those not conforming to a particular group's beliefs are stereotyped as demonstrated by the Catholic and Protestant divide. Group think, or to use a more recent expression, 'social compliance', is so persuasive that Christian communities will continue. As long as they hang on to old dogmas of dubious origin they will become increasingly irrelevant in the twenty-first century and gradually fade away. Tolstoy's epigraph at the beginning of this book reflects his deep understanding of the complex nature of human behaviour.

Works Cited

Armstrong, Karen, 1983, *The First Christian, St. Paul's Impact on Christianity* London: Pan Books.

Boardman, John (Ed.), 1986, *The Oxford History of the Classical World,* Oxford: Oxford University Press.

Bonhoeffer, Dietrich, 1960, (First pub. 1953), *Letters and Papers from Prison,* London: Fontana Books.

Casey, Maurice, 1991, *From Jewish Prophet to Gentile God,* Cambridge: James Clarke & Co.

Fredriksen, Paula, 1988, *From Jesus to Christ* Yale: Yale University Press.

Gibbon, Edward, 1963, *The Decline and Fall of the Roman Empire,* Middlesex: Penguin Books Ltd.

Handy, Charles, Fourth Ed. 1993, *Understanding Organisations,* London, Penguin Books Ltd.

Holland, Tom, 2004, *Rubicon The Triumph and Tragedy of the Roman Empire,* London: Abacus.

Holloway, Richard, *Godless Morality,* Edinburgh: Canongate Books Ltd.

Josephus, F., Trans. by William Whiston, 1862, *The Works of Flavius Josephus,* Halifax: Milner and Sowerby.

Montefiore, S. S, 2011, *Jerusalem, The Biography,* London: Orion Books Ltd.

O'Grady, S., 2012, *And Man Created God* London: Atlantic Books.

Pagels, Elaine, 1979, *The Gnostic Gospels,* London: Penguin Books.

Parke, H. W., 2004 (First Pub. 1988), *Sibyls and Sibylline Prophecy in Classical Antiquity ,* Abingdon: Routledge.

Pelikan, Jaroslav, 2005, *Whose Bible is it?* London: Penguin, Allen Lane.

Sanders, E. P., 1995, *The Historical Figure of Jesus* London: Penguin Books.

Schweitzer, Albert, 2005, (First pub. 1911) *The Quest of the Historical Jesus,* U.S.A: Dover Publications.

Stourton, Edward, 2004, *In the Footsteps of Saint Paul,* London: Hodder & Stoughton.

Tolstoy, Leo, (Ed. W. Gareth Jones), 2014, *What is art?* London: Bloomsbury.

Vermes, Geza, 1993, *The Religion of Jesus the Jew,* London: SCM Press.

—, 1994, *An Introduction to the Complete Dead Sea Scrolls,* London: SCM Press.

—, 2000, *The Changing Faces of Jesus,* London: Allen Lane.

—, 2001, (First pub. 1973), *Jesus the Jew,* London: SCM Press.

—, 2009 *Searching for the Real Jesus,* London: SCM Press.

Further Reading

Armstrong, Karen, 1993 *A History of God,* London: Mandarin Paperback.

—, 2007 *The Bible, The Biography* London: Atlantic Books.

Aslan, Reza, 2013, *Zealot The Life and Times of Jesus of Nazareth* London: The Westbourne Press.

Black, Matthew (Ed.), 1962, *Peake's Commentary on the Bible* London: Thomas Nelson & Sons.

Crossan, John Dominic, 1999, *The Birth of Christianity,* Edinburgh: T&T Clark Ltd.

Cupitt, Don, 1984, *The Sea of Faith,* London: British Broadcasting Corporation.

Dunn, James D. G., 1989, *Christology in the Making,* London: SCM Press.

Davies, Eryl W., 2010, *The Immoral Bible, Approaches to Biblical Ethics,* London: T & T Clark International.

Ehrman, Bart D., 2003, *Lost Scriptures,* Oxford: Oxford University Press.

Fredriksen, Paula, 1999, *Jesus of Nazareth, King of the Jews,* New York: Vintage Books.

Hick, John (Ed.), 1993 (Second Ed.), *The Myth of God Incarnate,* London: SCM Press Ltd.

Lawernce, T.E., 2014 (First pub. 1922) *Seven Pillars of Wisdom,* Great Britain: Burk Classics.

Manson, T.W., 1949, *The Sayings of Jesus,* London: SCM Press.

Pagels, Elaine, 2003, *Beyond Belief, the Secret Gospel of Thomas,* London: Macmillan.

Reza Aslan, 2013, *Zealot, The Life and Times of Jesus of Nazareth,* London: Westbourne Press.

Richardson, Alan (Ed.), 1958, *An Introduction to the Theology of the New Testament,* London: SCM Press Ltd.

Vermes, Geza, 2003, *The Authentic Gospel of Jesus,* London: Allen Lane.

—, 2005, *The Passion,* London: Penguin Books.

—, 2008, *The Resurrection*, London: Penguin Books.

Wiles, Maurice, 1967 *The Making of Christian Doctrine,* Cambridge: Cambridge University Press.

—, 1974, *The Remaking of Christian Doctrine,* London: SCM Press.

Williams, Rowan, 2003, *Resurrection,* London: Darton, Longman & Todd Ltd.

Wind, Renate, 1991, *A Spoke in the Wheel, The life of Dietrich Bonhoeffer,* London: SCM Press Ltd.

Zimmer, Carl, 2005, *Soul Made Flesh,* London: Arrow Books.